W9-CAE-747

DAVID ROSS was born near Glasgow at a very young age. He can trace his family tree back at least to the 1950s. For as long as he can remember he has had a passion for Scotland, its landscape, its traditions and its history. Every free moment is spent stravaiging around historic sites, battlefields and castles. He is a keen motorcyclist, as many x-rays can prove. He is looking forward to all the arguments that will take place in the forthcoming Scottish Parliament, showing that the Scots never change. He is 6ft 5in and naturally blond, although he is developing a distinguished touch of grey around the edges. He also has the audacity to think he looks the business in a kilt. His life is an ongoing quest for the truth, as if personally burdened by the bitter-sweet legacy of Wallace. His favourite current saying is 'Sorry – can't stop, I have a country to free'.

On the Trail of
William Wallace

DAVID R. ROSS

Luath Press Limited
EDINBURGH
www.luath.co.uk

First Edition 1999
Reprinted 1999

The paper used in this book is acid-free, neutral-sized and recyclable.
It is made from low chlorine pulps produced in a low energy,
low emission manner from sustainable forests.

Printed and bound by
Bell & Bain Ltd, Glasgow

Typeset in 10.5 point Sabon by
S. Fairgrieve, Edinburgh, 0131 658 1763

© David R. Ross

Wallace made Scotland. He is Scotland; he is the symbol of all that is best and purest and truest and most heroic in our national life. You cannot figure to yourself Scotland without Wallace. So long as grass grows green or water runs, or whilst the mist curls through the corries of the hills, the name of Wallace will live.

R B Cunninghame Graham

Acknowledgements

I would like to thank Karen and Kimberley; Linda Donnelly for all her hard work; Nigel Tranter for opening up another world to me when I was a teenager; Elspeth King; Bob McCutcheon for generously allowing me to reproduce photographs and illustrations from books in his extensive collection, in particular:

Vues Pittoresques de l'Écosse A Pichot (text), F.A. Pernot (engravings), 1827
Pictorial History of Scotland James Taylor, 1859
Border Antiquities of England and Scotland Walter Scott, 1814
Scotland Illustrated Dr William Beattie (text), T. Alcom, W.H. Bartlett and H. McCulloch (illustrations), 1838;

Anthony Fury for his line drawings; Jim Lewis for his maps and battle plans; Catriona Scott, editor; Gordon Ross; Harry Brydon, the Border Horseman; all at the Society of William Wallace, especially Irene and Duncan for their help – with a special mention for Willie Douglas, one of those people who works tirelessly for Scotland at no profit to himself; and to Shug Young – the bravest man I ever met.

Contents

Index Map   ix

Map A – East of Scotland   x

Map B – West of Scotland   xii

Map C – South East of Scotland and Northern England   xiv

Foreword   xvii

CHAPTER 1   The Reality   1

CHAPTER 2   Origins   4

CHAPTER 3   The National Situation   14

CHAPTER 4   Wallace – The Early Years   27

CHAPTER 5   Edward 1 of England – 'Longshanks'   38

CHAPTER 6   A More Concerted Effort   44

CHAPTER 7   The Turn of the Tide   56

CHAPTER 8   Stirling Bridge   67

CHAPTER 9   Invasion   78

CHAPTER 10   Falkirk   91

CHAPTER 11   Missions Abroad   103

CHAPTER 12   The Final Years   108

CHAPTER 13   The Last Days   112

CHAPTER 14   Edward's End   126

CHAPTER 15   Wallace Connections at Home and Abroad   131

CHAPTER 16   Wallace through the Ages   138

              Bibliography   144

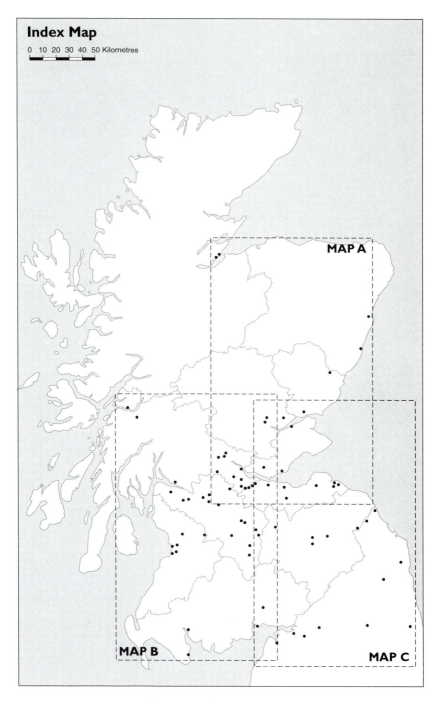

Index Map

0 10 20 30 40 50 Kilometres

MAP A

MAP B

MAP C

ix

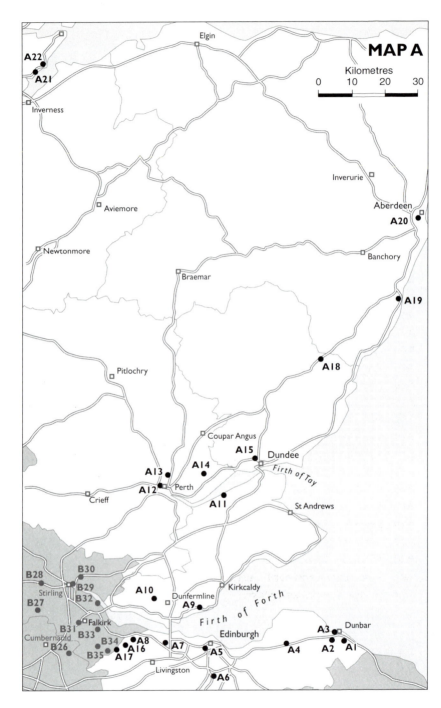

East of Scotland sites said to be connected with Wallace

Key to Map A

Ref		Page
A1	Innerwick: Wallace assailed the Earl of Dunbar.	81
A2	Spott: the Battle of Dunbar fought near here.	22
A3	Dunbar Castle: attacked by the English after the Sack of Berwick.	21
A4	Haddington: Wallace and Murray sent a letter from here.	79
A5	Edinburgh Castle: stained glass window of Wallace in St. Margaret's Chapel. Statue at castle entrance.	133
A6	Roslin: Scots won a battle 1303.	108
A7	Kirkliston: Edward camps.	94
A8	Linlithgow: Edward camps on Burghmuir before the Battle of Falkirk.	94
A9	Kinghorn: Alexander III monument.	16
A10	Dunfermline: Wallace's mother's grave.	90
A11	Lindores: site of battle of Black 'Ironside' or Earnside.	109
A12	Perth: Wallace slays soldiers.	47
A13	Scone: Wallace attacks Ormsby.	62
A14	Kilspindie: Wallace stays with uncle.	27
A15	Dundee: Wallace slays Selbie. Wallace plaque. Wallace schooled here.	28
A16	Cockleroy Hill: Wallace's Cradle on the summit.	94
A17	Torphichen: Scrymgeour letter written.	87
A18	Stracathro: Edward confronts Balliol in churchyard.	24
A19	Dunnottar: Wallace captures castle.	63
A20	Aberdeen: Wallace fires English shipping.	64
A21	Avoch: cairn marks north rising.	65
A22	Fortrose: Murray buried here.	76

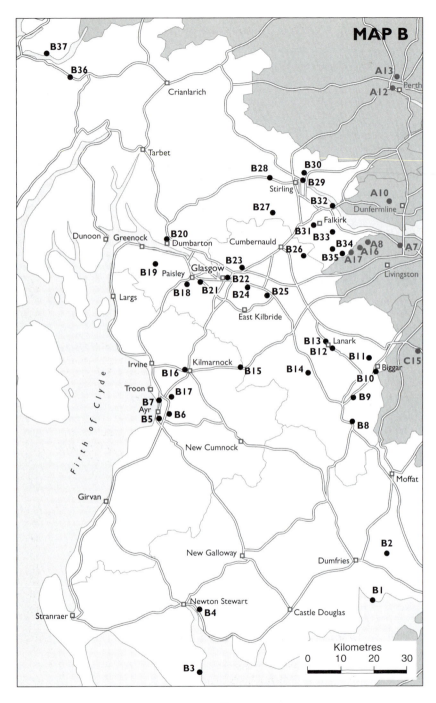

MAP B

B37
B36
Crianlarich
Tarbet
B28   B30
Stirling B29
B27   B32
Dunoon Greenock   Falkirk
B20   Cumbernauld B31 B33
Dumbarton   B34
B26   B35
B23
B19 Paisley Glasgow   B22
B18 B21   B24   B25
Largs   East Kilbride
A13
A12 Perth
A10
Dunfermline
A8
A16
A17   A7
Livingston

Irvine   Kilmarnock
B16   B15   B14
Troon B17
Ayr B7
B5 B6
B13 Lanark
B12
B11
B10 Biggar
B9
B8   C15

New Cumnock

Girvan   Moffat

New Galloway   B2
Dumfries

B1

Stranraer Newton Stewart   Castle Douglas
B4

Kilometres
0   10   20   30

B3

Firth of Clyde

West of Scotland sites said to be connected with Wallace

Key to Map B

Ref		Page
B1	Caerlaverock Castle: besieged by Edward.	107
B2	Lochmaben: castle taken by Wallace.	51
B3	Cruggleton Castle: Wallace makes an assault.	58
B4	Cree Estuary: Edward skirmished with the Scots.	107
B5	Ayr: The Barns of Ayr. Two Wallace statues.	34
B6	Auchencruive: a cairn to Wallace.	33
B7	Monkton: Wallace has a vision in a dream.	58
B8	Crawford or Lindsay Castle: burnt by Wallace.	52
B9	Lamington: home of Marion Braidfute.	53
B10	Biggar: Blind Harry has Wallace in battle.	57
B11	Quothquan: hill has a Wallace chair.	132
B12	Lanark: Wallace slew the sheriff. Wallace statue on the church.	51
B13	Kirkfieldbank: mentioned by Blind Harry. A Wallace oak stood here.	50
B14	Coalburn: Wallace cave.	46
B15	Loudoun Hill: Wallace fights battle. Site of Wallace's cairn.	44
B16	Riccarton: birthplace of Wallace's father. 'Bickering Bush' on Irvine Water	5
B17	Barnweill Hill: a monument to Wallace stands here.	60
B18	Elderslie: Wallace monument. Site of Wallace birthplace. Wallace oak and yew.	5
B19	Port Glasgow: site of tree where Wallace was chained.	117
B20	Dumbarton Castle: Wallace imprisoned.	115
B21	Paisley Abbey: Wallace educated. Wallace stained glass window.	31
B22	Glasgow: Battle of Bell o' the Brae. Wishart's tomb, Glasgow Cathedral	112
B23	Robroyston: Wallace captured 1305. Memorial and Wallace well.	113
B24	Rutherglen: Harry mentions church here.	58
B25	Bothwell Castle and Blantyre Priory.	65
B26	Wallace stone at Riggend.	92
B27	Dundaff: Sir John the Graham's castle.	50
B28	Gargunnock: Wallace attacks peel.	46
B29	Stirling: Wallace statue in town, Battle of Stirling Bridge	77
B30	National Wallace Monument.	67
B31	Dunipace: Wallace raised by his uncle here.	30
B32	Airth Castle: Wallace rescues his uncle, kills garrison.	88
B33	Falkirk: site of battle. Several monuments in town. Pillar at Wallace stone.	95
B34	Glen Ellrig: alternative Falkirk battle site. Standing stone.	101
B35	Wallace cave on river Avon.	103
B36	Pass of Brander: Wallace battle.	62
B37	Ardchattan Priory: Wallace holds council.	62

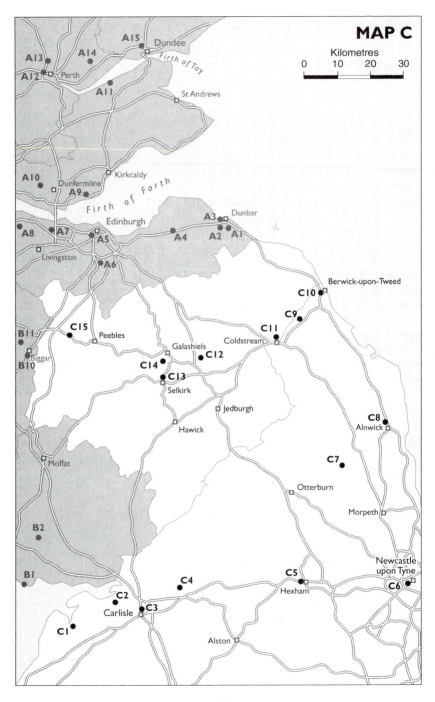

MAP C

Kilometres

0   10   20   30

A15 Dundee
Firth of Tay
A13 A14
A12 Perth
A11
St Andrews

A10 Kirkcaldy
Dunfermline
A9
Firth of Forth
A8 A7 A6
A5
Livingston
Edinburgh
A3 Dunbar
A4 A2 A1

Berwick-upon-Tweed
C10
C9
B11 C15 Peebles
C11 Coldstream
Biggar
B10 Galashiels
C14 C12
C13
Selkirk
Jedburgh
Hawick
C8
Alnwick
Moffat
C7
Otterburn
Morpeth
B2
Newcastle
upon Tyne
B1
C5 C6
C4 Hexham
C2
Carlisle C3
C1 Alston

xiv

South East of Scotland and Northern England sites said to be connected with Wallace

Key to Map C

Ref		Page
C1	Holm Cultram Abbey in Abbeytown: Edward's brain and entrails buried. Possibly visited by Wallace.	127
C2	Burgh by Sands: pillar marks where Edward Longshanks died.	127
C3	Carlisle Cathedral: Edward here in the days before his death.	127
C4	Lanercost Priory: visited by both Edward and Wallace.	84
C5	Hexham: Wallace wrote a letter of protection	82
C6	Newcastle: Wallace attacked the castle. One quarter of his body was sent here.	122
C7	Rothbury Forest: Wallace based his men here during the invasion of England.	82
C8	Alnwick: Wallace attacked the castle during the invasion of England.	82
C9	Norham Castle: Edward based here.	19
C10	Berwick: Edward sacked the town in 1296. One quarter of Wallace's body displayed.	20
C11	Coldstream: Edward invaded Scotland at the ford.	20
C12	Dryburgh: giant statue of Wallace on the hillside above the abbey.	134
C13	Selkirk: ruins of Kirk of the Forest where Wallace was perhaps created guardian.	86
C14	Caddonlea: where Scottish army mustered before the battle of Dunbar 1296.	21
C15	Happrew: Wallace defeated during his final years.	109

Foreword

IN 1998 I WAS lucky enough to attend the launch of the new edition of *Blind Harry's Wallace*. This account of the life of William Wallace is the second-biggest selling book ever in Scotland (the biggest being the Bible).

Elspeth King, a noted Wallace-ite, renowed for the excellent work she does in keeping Scotland's history alive at the Stirling Smith (and before that at the Abbot House in Dunfermline and The People's Palace in Glasgow) spoke at the launch. During her speech she said that she hoped someone someday would compile a list of all the Wallace-connected places mentioned in Blind Harry's work and elsewhere. This struck a chord in me.

As a teenager I became fascinated by the Scottish Wars of Independence (mostly Nigel Tranter's doing), and when I turned seventeen and purchased my first motorcycle, I started visiting the sites I had been reading about in history books. Although many bikes have come and gone, it never occurred to me that while I was enjoying myself, I was also amassing quite a bit of information. So, when Elspeth spoke about someone compiling a place list, I thought, 'I could do that'. This book is the result of my efforts.

Over the years, as my understanding of Scotland has grown, I have watched attitudes change in this little far-flung corner of Europe. We used to blunder along in Scotland like people who had lost their collective memory. But there seems to be a new awareness, a new dawning in the Scots, and no-one seems surprised any more when I tell them I am interested in Scotland's history, because so many people now are. It is not just the past which interests me, but I feel it is difficult to know your destination if you don't know where you came from.

Meanwhile, I will continue to enjoy the hilly countryside and the twisting turning roads that are so enjoyable on two wheels. I just wish it wasn't so bloody wet and cold.

David R Ross
January 1999

CHAPTER I

The Reality

WALLACE STEPPED FROM OBLIVION onto the pages of our history books a fully-grown man. Early in 1297, he slew the Sheriff of Lanark, and the spark of rebellion was ignited. Young men of like mind flocked to his banner. He joined forces with Andrew Murray, who had sparked a similar rebellion in the north of Scotland, and together they defeated an English army at Stirling Bridge; unfortunately Murray was wounded during the battle and he died later that year. Wallace went on to invade northern England, but was beaten back by the early onset of a hard winter. He returned to Scotland and was created Guardian.

In the following year, Edward Plantagenet, 'Longshanks', King of England, brought his army north, to teach the Scots a lesson. The two armies met on a hillside near Falkirk where, after a bloody battle, the Scots were defeated with great losses. Wallace resigned the Guardianship, and from then until his capture seven years later, the details of his life are sketchy. It is known that he went to France, and perhaps to Rome, to plead Scotland's case to the Pope. On his return home, he fought against increasingly overwhelming odds. His last action of which we have a record, was a skirmish at 'Black Ironside' in September 1304. He was captured near Glasgow in August 1305 and taken to London where he was barbarously executed.

These scant details are all we really have to tell us the story of Wallace's life. Copies of letters Wallace issued during his brief Guardianship have survived, and these, at least, give us some insight into the man and his whereabouts when they were written. Most of the extra factual details are gleaned from English records or chronicles; for instance, the record of his trial tells of his slaying of the Sheriff of Lanark. Everything else we know comes from later chronicles, folktales, and the work of Blind Harry.

Blind Harry lived in the 1400s and wrote an epic poem extolling the virtues of Wallace. Much of it is based on reality, but much is fantasy. It has been ignored by most historians as there are no other documents to back it up, but it is an essential tool in letting us see how the ordinary Scot has viewed Wallace down the ages. The fact that many old histories, records and gazetteers make reference to the work of Harry shows just how popular this book has been with generations of Scots over the centuries.

In reality, there are two William Wallaces – the Wallace of history and the Wallace of legend. They have combined to become a symbol of hope for Scots down through the ages. And not only Scots. Throughout the world many people who cherish the concept of freedom have adopted Wallace or his ideals.

What I have set out to do in this book is take the bare bones of the historical Wallace's life and flesh them out with the Wallace of legend to give a picture of the life of this remarkable man. It will also act as a guide book, which people with an interest in Wallace can use to discover where incidents in his life took place, and even visit them. But, most of all, I hope that it will encourage others to follow and build on the research that I have done so far.

In the text, where I am giving hard facts, I will state that this is so. Similarly, when relating folktales or legend, I will point this out. Some of the stories come from people who live near certain sites linked to Wallace and have passed on local legend to me, and others are mere conjecture: I hope the difference will be obvious. A few of the stories have very tenuous links indeed with the reality of Wallace, but the fact that people believe, or at least know of, them means that they are worth recording, even if just to see how Wallace is viewed at the very end of the 20th century. Perhaps in the future new evidence will come to light to back up some of the more exotic tales.

Whatever the truth of the stories, Wallace died for Scotland's sins, and his example has shone like a beacon through the centuries for every generation of Scots men and women who cherish notions of freedom. When times have been difficult, his selfless devotion and love of his native soil have proved inspirational. His influence still stands like a shadow falling over modern Scotland – the fact that a referendum on the future of this small nation took place in 1997 on the 700th anniversary of the Battle of Stirling Bridge testifies to that. There is little doubt that the Wallace of legend will continue to be re-invented to inspire future generations.

CHAPTER 2

Origins

DAVID I OF SCOTLAND was born in the year 1084. He was the son of Malcolm Canmore, King of Scots, and Margaret Atheling who introduced the Roman Catholic faith to Scotland, and who was later to be canonised as St Margaret. David was a great church builder, as the Border Abbeys will testify, and he began the process of minting the first Scottish coinage. He spent much of his time south of the border where he was impressed by the Norman style of feudalism.

When he became King in 1124, he began to invite Norman families into his realm, thereby introducing a military presence never before seen in this northern kingdom. He gave them land and rank, and through time they became the great families of Scotland. Among many illustrious names who came north were three who would later become the ruling houses of Scotland. The Balliols were granted land in Galloway, the Bruces were given the title Lords of Annandale, and the Fitz-Alans were granted lands in Renfrew and the Kyle district of Ayrshire and became the Hereditary Stewards of the kingdom. These Stewards of David I would eventually form the Stewart dynasty, who would in the course of time also inherit the throne of England, as James the Sixth and First.

When the Fitz-Alans came north from Shropshire on the Welsh marches, they brought with them as their vassals (men in their service) a family by the name of Walays. This was the English for a Celt or a Welshman. These Walays or Wallaces were granted some lands by the Stewards to run on their behalf. When Walter Fitz-Alan founded the great abbey of Paisley in 1163, the charter confirming this was witnessed by a certain Richard Wallace, a man regarded as being an ancestor of William Wallace.

The Wallaces soon held estates in various parts of the Kyle district of Ayrshire, which is the portion between the Rivers Irvine and Doon. The area north of the River Irvine is called Cunningham, and that south of the River Doon is called Carrick. The importance of this information will become obvious when the location of Wallace's birthplace is discussed.

The Wallaces also held lands in Renfrewshire – Blind Harry says that Wallace's father held the lands of Elderslie and Auchenbothie there. Although there is no hard evidence of the Wallaces holding Elderslie before 1390, it is certainly possible that they did so from a much earlier date – but at least we know that Elderslie was a Wallace property. (MAP B18)

The Wallaces held Riccarton (now a suburb of Kilmarnock) in the Kyle district of Ayrshire, and many writers have stated that this spot was named after the Richard Wallace mentioned above (Richards-tun, or manor, therefore Riccarton). This is conjecture, but it is probable that this is how it got its name. (MAP B16)

Legend states that Wallace's father was born at Riccarton, the spot now crowned by the parish church. A small granite plaque at the entrance to Riccarton Fire Station testifies to this. It states:

Site of Riccarton Castle
Birthplace of Malcolm Wallace
Father of 'Scotland's Hero'.

The plaque was originally located nearer the old 'moot-hill' site where the church now stands, but was moved during the course of various road-widening operations and is now inserted in a little brick structure designed to house it.

Riccarton Church

Even Wallace's father's name is open to question. The Scotichronicon is a chronicle of Scotland composed in the 1440s, and where it mentioned Wallace's father, the space was left blank. Later hands have written 'Malcolm' in one version and 'Andrew' in another. Blind Harry gives Wallace's mother as Margaret Crauford of Corsbie, a small estate near Troon, but there is no hard evidence to back this up.

A Gazetteer of Scotland published in 1842 has an interesting entry with the following excerpt on Riccarton:

> Sir Ronald Crawford, the maternal uncle of Sir William Wallace, had, in this parish, a residence to which his illustrious nephew often resorted, and whence he sallied to perform many of the exploits which fame assigns him in the tales of tradition. The residence is said to have been a tower on the site of the farm-house of Yardsides, immediately west of the village, but is has entirely disappeared, and has left, even in its vicinity, very doubtful memorials. A very ruinous and very humble edifice at the west end of a

little row of cottages beside the farm-house is pointed out as the barn which belonged to the tower, and, respectively in the garden and at the entrance to the farm yard are a pear-tree which Wallace is said to have personally planted, and a very old tree perforated with an iron staple to which he fastened his horse when he visited the tower.

One fact of which we are sure is that Wallace was the middle of three brothers, the elder being Malcolm and the younger John. We know of their existence because they are mentioned in English chronicles. All three brothers were eventually to be executed at the hands of the English. Blind Harry mentions two sisters, but we know little about them.

On the question of Wallace's birthplace, Blind Harry states that Wallace's father was 'Malcolm Wallace then of Ellerslie'. It is worth noting that on various maps through the ages Elderslie in Renfrewshire is named either Elderslie or Ellerslie, both variations of 'field of the elder trees'. In the original old Scots version of Blind Harry, it is written as 'Elrisle', i.e. El-ris-lee. Elderslie has long been famous as the traditional birthplace of Wallace.

From the first owner whose name is on record in 1390 (although it is believed the family owned these lands as early as the beginning of the 13th century), the property remained in the hands of succeeding generations of Wallaces, twelve in total. The only child of the twelfth generation was a beauty by the name of Helen Wallace who married one Archibald Campbell of Succoth and Garscube. Helen eventually sold the Elderslie estate to Alexander Speirs, a merchant in Glasgow, and it subsequently passed through several generations of the Speirs family.

Alexander Speirs was responsible for the building of the Church of St Andrews by the Green in Glasgow, where he had a plaque erected by the altar which stated that he had 'bought the lands of Elderslie from a descendant of William Wallace'. This church still stands at the side of Glasgow Green, but before its current use as offices, it lay derelict for several years, and unfortunately the plaque was either destroyed or disappeared.

The current owners of Elderslie estate are the Crichton-Maitland family, under the moniker of the Elderslie and Houston estates.

Several interesting relics of the Wallace era can be seen in the village of Elderslie. A map drawn by Pont in the 1500s shows Elderslie as a fenced stronghold by the Alt Patrick Water. In the late 1700s a stone was discovered in the garden of this building which bore the inscription 'W.W.W. Christ is only my redeemer'. These initials are believed to refer to William Wallace, father and son, who had inherited the property in the 1500s.

Part of the building was still standing until the 1970s, when the bulk of it was demolished. Surely it would have been worth saving to use as some type of Wallace heritage centre, to provide education as well as giving the village of Elderslie a focal point. It is hard to think of any other country in the world destroying a building that had such a strong connection with its national hero. All that now remains are a few low walls near the modern memorial.

The building either occupied or was close to the site of the original property from Wallace's day. The house which now stands just south of the modern memorial, on the rising ground above the Alt Patrick Water, is intriguingly named the Moat House. This is probably a corruption of moot-house, the term in medieval times for a fortified dwelling. In the gardens of the property are some traces of defensive earthworks, and in the surrounding wall there are interesting stones which obviously come from an older building.

On a stretch of grassland nearby stands an old yew tree. Parish records from the 1700s refer to it as 'this ancient tree', so it is possible that it dates back to Wallace's time. It is certainly known locally as the Wallace Yew, but this is probably because of its situation.

A more famous tree once stood on the north side of the main road, just by the Alt Patrick Water, on a site now covered by a restaurant building. This was the famous Wallace Oak which was reputed to have once hidden Wallace and 300 of his followers from an English patrol. This is patently untrue, as Wallace, backed by 300 followers, would not have been a man to hide up a tree! The Wallace connection, however, is old and widely known. The followers of Bonnie Prince Charlie during the 1745 rebellion used the words 'The Wallace Oak' as a camp password, and proof of this still exists in the camp orders.

The tree was once measured and its branches were estimated to cover 495 square yards, but time and relic-mongers eventually reduced it to a shadow of its former self, and it finally fell in a storm in February 1856. I have seen several artefacts that were carved from its wood including snuff-boxes, writing boxes and even one or two images of Wallace himself. Before it fell, an acorn from the tree was grown to a sapling, which was later planted in the Fountain Gardens in Paisley, where it thrived. There are four oaks in the Fountain Gardens, and after many enquiries to ascertain which was the descendent of the Wallace Oak, I eventually found out that it is the one in the north-west corner of the garden.

Approaching the site of the Wallace house from the Paisley direction, there is a small stone edifice on the north side of the road. This is old well known locally as the Bore Well due to the fact that its waters permeate up through an old mine bore. The well is surmounted by a stone cup which represents the 'Cup of Freedom', a reference to Wallace's life work. (Water from the well is perfectly clear, but when it is added to whisky in the fittingly named Wallace Tavern across the road, it discolours the spirit, turning it a shade of grey. This is caused by minerals in the water.)

Wallace Well, Elderslie

The Elderslie Wallace Monument is a beautiful granite edifice, the foundation stone of which was laid on 15 June, 1912. The money for the monument was raised by the London Renfrewshire Association, under the guidance of Mr A Skene Smith, who had been a native of the district. Donations came from many quarters, and the monument, which cost £2,000, was officially unveiled on 28 September, 1912, before a crowd of some 4,000 to 5,000 people.

Plaques depicting scenes from Wallace's life were to have been installed on the monument at this time, but the committee ran out of funds. They were eventually added in 1970, the money having come from the Clan

Elderslie Monument

Wallace Society of the United States of America. Four of the six plaques are exquisitly detailed and illustrate: Wallace leading the Scots at Stirling Bridge, Wallace raising the Scottish standard, Wallace receiving the Guardianship of Scotland, and Wallace showing Bruce the error of his ways after Falkirk. The other two are copies of plaques in London, one in the floor of Westminster Hall marking the spot where Wallace was tried, and the other at Smithfield where his murder took place.

The monument is a local landmark and stands within a grassy area, a magnet for local youths and unfortunately the object of vandalism. Before the annual Wallace Day, which takes place on the weekend closest to the date of his death, the monument has to be thoroughly cleaned. The celebrations include a march from Johnstone into Elderslie after which speeches are made.

Many historians are of the opinion that Elderslie was the place of Wallace's birth: all the evidence points in that direction. But as there were no birth certificates in Wallace's time, there will always be room for conjecture as to his birthplace.

The Wallace family held many properties in the Kyle district of Ayrshire, and over the years there have been several claims for an Ayrshire birthplace. Although we cannot be certain as to his birthplace, we should at least be able to dismiss the inaccurate. Hopefully, the following observations will help to give some pointers to the reality of the situation.

Various claims have centred around Craigie Castle, the ruins of which stand near Craigie village. Although Craigie was a famous Wallace seat, it did not become so until 1371, when a certain John Wallace married the Lindsay heiress, thereby bringing the castle under his family's control. As the Wallace of this investigation was born a century before this, it is obviously impossible for Craigie to have any connecton with his place of birth.

Much controversy has arisen recently regarding Ellerslie near Kilmarnock, with one writer going as far as naming it Wallace's birthplace. This Ellerslie was a large house attached to a small works and some cottages, and does not appear on any map before 1850. (It should be borne in mind that Ayrshire is one of the best mapped areas of Scotland.) This particular Ellerslie was constructed by a Mr Finnie who stayed in nearby Springhill, and he leased the land from the Duke of Portland. Mr Finnie was a Kilmarnock councillor. One of his colleagues was named William Wallace, and it is not unreasonable to think that he may have had a hand in naming these cottages 'Ellerslie'. Ellerslie house still stands, but the cottages and works have long gone. The land reverted to the Duke of Portland, and remained in his family's possession until the 1960s.

The reason for the confusion surrounding this site is created by old documents referring to 'The five pound land of Ellerslie in the parish of Riccarton' which has caused some to look for an Ayrshire Ellerslie, and this one has been made to fit the bill. However, it does not stand in Riccarton parish, but in Kilmaurs parish. Riccarton parish is in Kyle, and this building is on the other side of the River Irvine in Cunningham.

What has been overlooked is that the Renfrewshire Elderslie – the traditional birthplace of Wallace – was 'farmed out' to Riccarton parish from the Abbey Parish of Paisley. This fact is preserved in the Elderslie title-deeds. No date is given for this, but it was certainly before 1678. Elderslie remained in

Riccarton parish until 1747, when it returned to Paisley Abbey parish, put back in place by Act 20, George II, cap.43, which abolished heritable jurisdictions.

One other factor which must be taken into account is that the Stewards, and therefore the Wallaces as their vassals, never had land in Cunningham district, further proof that this area as a birthplace is an impossibility.

Complex as all this is, it must be recorded. Mistakes need only be made in source material once for them to be repeated in later works.

Many of the claims for an Ayrshire birthplace appear to emanate from Ayrshire itself. And who could blame people for wanting to attach themselves to a national hero? Ayrshire already 'has' Bruce and Burns, so it is just the thing for the area to want the trinity! It is worth noting that Burns, who was inspired by Wallace and admired him greatly, never claimed an Ayrshire birthplace for him.

But does it really matter where William Wallace was born? In a word – no. It is the deeds of the grown man that count. All I have tried to do is convey information, because so much controversy has arisen around the subject. The march will still take place every year at Elderslie. The memorial stands in Elderslie because this is the spot where Wallace is believed to have been born. It is a good thing that such a memorial exists, and that's good enough for me!

CHAPTER 3

The National Situation

WHEN WALLACE WAS BORN, Alexander III had been King of Scots for many years. Alexander was born in 1241, and had reigned since 1249. Scotland was in a fairly stable condition. Many coins survive from Alexander's reign which shows that economically, things were going well. Peace was the order of the day and the Scots were able to till the land and reap their harvests unmolested. Later generations would look back on Alexander's reign as 'the good old days'.

War was virtually unknown, and there had been no fighting in Scotland since the Battle of Largs in 1263, when Alexander's men defeated a Norse fleet under King Hakon, and gained control of the Isle of Man and the Western Isles, in what was, in reality, little more than a major skirmish. A monument to this battle known locally as 'the pencil' stands at the southern end of modern Largs.

Alexander's first wife was Margaret of England, sister to Edward Plantagenet – Longshanks. She died in 1275 and had borne two sons and a daughter, but Alexander outlived them all. His nearest relative was his grand-daughter Margaret. (His own daughter had lived long enough to marry the King of Norway, but she had died in childbirth.) This little girl is better known to history as The Maid of Norway. She was a sickly child, and in medieval times a country like Scotland demanded a strong male as a ruler. If a young girl were on the throne, factions would form which would manipulate the situation for their own ends.

Scotland needed a male heir, and in 1285 Alexander married Yolande, daughter of the Comte de Dreux. They had been married less than a year before disaster overtook Alexander. Even in his wildest dreams he could never have imagined how much his death would change his kingdom. Scotland was going to be hammered into shape, as if on an anvil, and the hammer was to be Alexander's brother-in-law, Edward of England. The personality of the Scots would change because of this, and 700 years later memory would still have them eyeing Englishmen with suspicion.

On the afternoon of Monday, 18 March, 1286, Alexander set out from Edinburgh Castle, determined to reach Kinghorn, which could normally be seen across the Firth of Forth, but that day the weather was particularly bad. Yolande was at Kinghorn Castle, and during that day's session with his council, Alexander's mind must have been on his young French bride. He made his way to Dalmeny, where he had to persuade the ferryman to take him and his few men-at-arms across the two miles of stormy water to Inverkeithing. Legend has it that when Alexander asked the ferryman if he was afraid, the man replied, 'I could do worse than die in the company of your father's son'.

He was met on the other side of the Forth by Alexander, Master of the Royal Sauce-kitchen, who also rebuked him, asking him not to travel further, but he could not be dissuaded. He never reached

Kinghorn Monument

Kinghorn, for somewhere in the dark

his escort lost sight of him, and in the morning he was found dead, his neck broken. His horse must have stumbled, and thrown him over a cliff. The spot where he lay was marked with a stone cross, which was replaced by a larger monument in 1886. This stands on the south side of the coast road between Burntisland and Kinghorn, at Pettycur Bay. Nothing now remains of the castle at Kinghorn, which stood on rising ground to the north of the town. (MAP A9)

One of Scotland's oldest poems describes this tragedy:

When Alexander our King was dead
That Scotland led in love and law
Away was sons (plenty) of ale and bread
Of wine and wax, of game and glee
Our gold was changed into lead
Christ, born in virginity
Succour Scotland, and remedy
That State is in perplexity.

Alexander was buried in Dunfermline Abbey beside his first wife, Margaret. The people of Scotland waited with bated breath, in the hope that Yolande might be pregnant with an heir, but it was not to be. Yolande disappears from our history books at this point, and we can only assume she returned to France.

As these events were taking place, William Wallace was probably about twelve. People would be gossiping and wondering what the future held, and it is easy to imagine the news spreading through the country, and Wallace hearing that the king was dead.

Scotland's eyes turned to Norway and the little girl there who was now the uncrowned queen. At this point Edward of

England suddenly took an interest in Scotland's affairs, and embroiled himself in dealings where the Maid of Norway was concerned. He sent a ship to Norway to carry her across the North Sea. The provisions on board included figs, raisins and gingerbread – the sweets of the day. Without really considering the wishes of Scotland, he had proposed a treaty whereby the little Maid should be married to his son (the future Edward II) who had been born in 1284. Margaret's father, Erik II of Norway, dismissed Edward's ship, insisting that one of his own would be used. Eric knew that Edward would have had his ship sail straight to London, a situation which would have made Scotland subordinate to him.

At this time Edward also took control of the Isle of Man which Alexander had won control of after the Battle of Largs. But most sinister was Edward's appointment of Anthony Beck, Bishop of Durham, to be Lieutenant of Scotland in the name of his son and the Maid, even though they had not yet been married.

The news of the Maid of Norway's death spread through Scotland in October 1290. She had reached Orkney, and had apparently died there in the arms of Bishop Narve of Bergen. She was only seven. Her body was taken back to Bergen to be buried in the cathedral, but not before her father opened the coffin to make sure the body was that of his daughter. (There is a bizarre postcript to this tragic story. After Erik died, a young German woman from Lübeck arrived in Norway in 1300, claiming she was the Maid. She was put on trial and found to be an imposter, and was burned to death in Bergen.)

The Maid of Norway was also the heiress to the throne of Norway, and it is interesting to speculate on what might have transpired if she had lived. Would there have been some kind of union between Scotland and Norway, forming a trans-North Sea power? Edward of England may have thought of this when he tried to arrange the Maid's marriage to his son, in the hope that England's larger population would give it the means to be overlord to both. It must be borne in mind that, as is the case still, there were approximately ten English for every Scot. In Wallace's time, Scotland was a country of perhaps half a million souls to England's five million. Today the ratio is the same – five million Scots to fifty million English.

There was no straightforward heir to the throne of Scotland. and thirteen claimants came forward, all saying that they should rightfully be king. There were no legitimate heirs, until we trace the royal line of Scotland back to the time of Malcolm the Maiden and his brother, William the Lion. Neither left heirs, but their younger brother, David, Earl of Huntingdon, had three daughters. John Balliol was the grandson of the eldest daughter, and Robert Bruce (grandfather of the victor at Bannockburn) was the son of the second daughter. These two had the most legitimate claim to the throne.

Although Balliol appeared to have a better claim, being descended from the elder daughter, things were not that straight-forward. There was real threat of civil war in Scotland, for if Balliol tried to mount the throne, the Bruce faction would bitterly contest it, and vice versa, not to mention the demands of some the other claimants. Only one person could choose the king and stop the others quarrelling, and that was another king.

In a bid to stop blood being shed, Bishop Fraser of St Andrews wrote to Edward asking for his intervention. There was no lack of patriotism in this act, for after all, Edward was the brother-in-law of the late King Alexander and had been ready to marry his son to the Maid of Norway. Edward

Norham Castle

happily came north to pick the rightful heir to the Scottish throne. He reached Norham Castle on the English side of the Tweed in May 1291, and called the Scots to meet him there to settle the dispute. (MAP C9) When they arrived, he demanded that they should accept his suzerainty, ie. his overlord-ship. Professor Barrow, in his work on Bruce, puts it succinctly when he states that Edward did not ask the Scots, 'Am I the rightful suzerain of Scotland', but put the question, 'Can you produce any evidence to show that I am not the rightful suzerain of Scotland'.

The claimants all acknowledged Edward as their feudal superior – ambition had overridden any right thinking where Scotland was concerned. Edward together with his advisers deliberated long and hard, and in November 1292 he announced that John Balliol was heir to the throne of Scotland. It was the correct decision, for Balliol was descended from the eldest daughter of David, Earl of Huntingdon. He was crowned on St Andrew's Day, 30 November, 1292.

History has not been kind to John Balliol; he was outshone by Bruce, but he did his best against overwhelming odds. Edward immediately began to bully him, and to make humiliating demands on him at every turn. For example, he demanded that the Scots army be mustered for military service to fight in England's wars in France. Eventually the worm turned, and in 1295 Balliol resigned his homage to Edward, and went into alliance with France. This was the beginning of the 'Auld Alliance' between Scotland and France, where the two nations would unite to try to counter aggressive English threats. The Wars of Independence was about to begin.

The English army at this time was the greatest fighting machine in Christendom. Its soldiers were seasoned campaigners, its captains were veterans of Edward's continental wars. It made its way to the River Tweed, and crossed at the ford at the point where the Coldstream enters the Tweed from the Scottish side. The river course seems to have changed little since, and one can stand on the grassland on the Scottish bank, right on the spot where many years of warfare were then about to begin. (MAP C11)

Once across the river, the English army turned east and marched downstream towards Berwick on Tweed. At this time Berwick was the largest town in Scotland. It did a vast amount of trade with European ports, exporting sheepskins from the Lammermuir Hills inland from the coast. Celtic art was in high demand on the Continent, and exports were booming. Foreign traders had bases in Berwick. The merchants of Cologne had their own 'factory' by the name of the White Hall. The Flemings had an equivalent called the Red Hall which they held on the agreement that they would always defend it against English aggression.

Edward arrived before Berwick on 30 March, 1296. (MAP C10) The town was protected by ditches and turf and timber palisades. The dragon banner was unfurled. In medieval times this banner meant that there would be no mercy and no prisoners taken. The English smashed into Berwick at the first assault, Edward astride his favourite horse, a black charger called Bayard. The townsfolk were slaughtered by the soldiers. The merchants in the Red Hall were burnt to death doing their best to defend it. The slaughter was said to have continued for three days, with Edward only calling a halt when he saw one of his soldiers butchering a woman in the act of childbirth.

Berwick had been a town with 20,000 inhabitants. How many survived the carnage is not known. The English chronicles reported huge numbers of dead, and a realistic figure might be some 12,000 to 15,000. Today the population of Berwick is only 12,000, so the town never recovered its former glory.

Southern eyes had coveted this Scottish town for a long time for it was said to do as much trade as a quarter of all the ports of England together. Edward began to settle the town with people from south of the border, and in the long run this had the desired effect, for Berwick is now an English town. Edward also began to strengthen the town walls, building them in stone, and parts of these can be seen to this day, leading from the railway station down to the River Tweed. These walls should not be confused with the later town walls which were built in Elizabethan times.

After the sacking of Berwick, Edward and his army turned north and started to advance into Scotland. The Scots had not lain dormant. They had assembled their 'feudal host' at Caddonlea which had long been a gathering place for Scottish armies. Caddonlea stands on the River Tweed between Walkerburn and Melrose at the point where the Caddon Water enters the Tweed. The tiny village nearby is named Caddonfoot. (MAP C14)

The Scots marched east from here, and made their way towards Dunbar, which the English army was now besieging. (MAP A3) On Friday, 27 April, 1296 the Scottish army appeared on the heights inland from Dunbar and the besiegers immediately turned to the attack. To reach the Scots, they had to drop into the valley of the Spott Burn. (MAP A2) In their ignorance of warfare, the Scots thought the English army was beginning to break up. They charged piecemeal down the hillside, only to fall headlong into the English troops who were ranked in good order. Most of the notable names on the Scottish side were captured, and many ordinary foot-soldiers were slain. The army of Scotland was broken in a matter of minutes, leaving the country defenceless.

Only scant remains of the once mighty fortress still stand at Dunbar harbour. It was built across several rock stacks standing in the North Sea, joined together by stone causeways or bridges. Recently one of these bridges collapsed, and each year it becomes harder to discern just how formidable this place once was.

Langtoft's chronicle relates a popular song which was sung in England after this battle, perhaps as a soldiers' marching song. Loosely translated, it runs:

For those Scots
I rate 'em as sots
What a sorry shower!
Whose utter lack
In the attack
Lost 'em at Dunbar.

Modern ordnance survey maps show the site of this battle in a field above the Spott Burn. It should not be confused with a battle fought in this area at a much later date.

It is just possible that William Wallace was present at the Battle of Dunbar. After all, his first step onto the pages of our history books at Lanark was only a year away. At the time of

Dunbar he would have been in his early twenties. If he was not there, his brother Malcolm may have been, and this would certainly have given either man first-hand knowledge of trained English soldiers, which would have proved helpful later at the Battle of Stirling Bridge.

After Dunbar, the invaders moved north through Edinburgh and Stirling, and Edward began to try to strip Scotland of her nationhood. He had the Scottish records shipped to London, together with many other valuables including the Holy or Black Rood of St Margaret. This was an icon of the Scottish people, brought to Scotland by St Margaret, and believed to be a piece of the cross on which Christ was crucified. Rood is the old Scots for a cross, and Holyrood in Edinburgh takes its name from this.

No-one knows what became of the Black Rood. Some reports say that it was returned to Scotland after the Wars of Independence and carried into battle by Bruce's son, David II, when it was again captured at the Battle of Neville's Cross. It was then taken to Durham Cathedral and shown as a spoil of war, only to disappear during the Reformation. Other reports say that it never returned from London.

The Stone of Destiny, the ancient crowning stone of the Kings of Scots, was also sent south, to prove that the nation of Scotland no longer existed. Legend said that wherever the Stone stood, from there Scotland would be ruled. For 700 years it remained in Westminster Abbey, and as a boy I stood in the Abbey, looking at it out of reach behind iron railings, with a sign on the wall which said:

The Stone of Scone
Brought here by Edward I
To show Scotland's subservience.

I also stood above the bridge at Coldstream 700 years after it had crossed here going south, to watch it come home in 1996. A year later Scotland voted to take some pride in itself again, and set up some sort of parliament, so perhaps the legend connected with the Stone is true. Wallace's shadow still hangs over Scotland – I see wrongs being righted and what must be history in the making. However, if Wallace's shadow is still there, Edward's is too.

King Edward continued to march northwards to confront Balliol, who by this time was a fugitive in the North and South Esk Glens in Angus. He was caught and brought

Stracathro Church

before Edward in the small churchyard at Stracathro, a few miles north of Brechin. (MAP A18) There is still a small church here on what must be an ancient site, and it is moving to stand in the churchyard where Edward forced Balliol to renounce his treaty with France. There is nothing there today to connect it with those times, but if one knows its history, it is a poignant spot.

The following day, in Montrose, Balliol was stripped of the Crown of Scotland. To his humiliation, his Lion Rampant surcoat was also stripped from him, which earned him the nickname 'Toom Tabard', or 'empty coat'. He was sent south to the Tower of London, and was later moved to Hertford.

This took place on 8 July, 1296, which meant that from that day there was no King of Scots. Edward had assumed power, and to demonstrate this, he marched onwards through Scotland, eventually travelling as far as Elgin.

Leaving lieutenants to oversee the conquest, Edward moved south again and based himself at Berwick, where he demanded that the landed gentry of Scotland come and sign a document declaring fealty to him as their overlord. As landowners arrived from all over Scotland, Berwick's condition after the massacre would be plain to all, and a poignant reminder of Edward's power. Most of the upper classes seemed ready to do whatever was needed to push their own interests to the fore, and as Edward's star was in the ascendancy, they were quite willing to sign the document.

Many Scots, however, must have been moved by patriotic feelings, and they would take the view that their signatures to the document were forced under duress. Two names are conspicuous by their absence. William Wallace's name does not appear, nor, more surprisingly, that of his elder brother Malcolm, who would by this time have inherited the Elderslie estate. This would be in keeping with Wallace's, and probably Malcolm's, attitude towards Engish occupation, for, whereas many of the nobility would do whatever was in their own best interest at the time, Wallace would never bend his knee to any usurption of his beloved country.

The document became known to history as the 'Ragman's Roll', a reference to the state of the downtrodden Scots who signed it. The name has come down through the years, in the form of the word 'rigmarole', meaning something that is time-consuming and worthless. The castle at Berwick where it was signed was still standing in the 1800s, but it was mostly demolished to make way for the railway station. A few bits remain, at the far side of the station.

Edward now had many of the ruling families, who had not been captured at Dunbar, taken captive. Among them was a name we should bear in mind: Andrew Murray, heir of Petty in Invernessshire, Avoch in the Black Isle and Boharm in Banffshire. He was held captive at Chester.

Meanwhile, to ensure English rule in Scotland, the victor of Dunbar, Warenne, was made keeper, Hugh Cressingham was made treasurer, and Walter of Amersham, chancellor. William Ormsby became chief justiciar. Edward then made his way south, and it is reported that as he crossed the Tweed, he turned and remarked to his captains, 'It does a man good to be rid of a turd'.

He had no idea that once he was over the border, many who had declared their fealty to him would denounce him, and although he had imprisoned many of the ruling families of Scotland, in her hour of need a defender would arise. For William Wallace was about to raise his head.

The Coronation Chair at Westminster
This old print shows the Coronation Chair containing the Stone of Destiny, looted
from Scone by Edward Longshanks.

Berwick Castle

Berwick was the scene of the infamous 'Sack of Berwick', the signing of the 'Ragmans Roll', and part of Wallace's remains was displayed here. The Castle was mostly destroyed in victorian times to make way for the railway station.

Lanark Castle
Here Wallace slew Heselrig the English Sheriff. The site is now a bowling green.

Dunbar Castle
The scant ruins of Dunbar – a mighty fortress in Wallace's day, stand above the harbour in the town of the same name.

Dunfermline Abbey

Legend states Wallace's mother is buried within the churchyard. There is also a stained glass window of Wallace by Sir Noel Paton.

Dunnottar Castle

This castle on its stack of rock south of Stonehaven was fired by Wallace.

Loch Awe

Wallace fought at the Pass of Brander, the pass containing the North-West arm of the Loch.

Letters in support of the National Wallace Monument, 1868.
This set, including a letter from Garibaldi, is framed in wood from the Wallace oak.
It is on display at the Stirling Smith Art Gallery and Museum.

The Wallace Tower in Ayr

Scone

Wallace made a raid here. The Cross is all that remains from the Old Town.

CHAPTER 4

Wallace – The Early Years

NO SOLID FACTS ARE KNOWN of Wallace's life before Lanark and his murder of Hesilrig, its Sheriff. We must use the work of Blind Harry for most of our knowledge of his early days. Harry's dates are sometimes somewhat out of kilter, but it is possible to construct a brief outline of the main points.

When English soldiers began to garrison Scotland, Wallace's father decided that things were becoming a little hot for him, and he took Wallace's elder brother, Malcolm, to the Lennox, the area around southern Loch Lomond. Wallace's mother took William to stay with an old uncle at Kilspindie in the Carse of Gowrie, on the north shore of the Firth of Tay. (MAP A14) In ancient times there was a castle at Kilspindie, but no trace of it has survived. While in residence there, Wallace attended school in Dundee. Wallace grew to manhood, and was 'seemly, strapping, stout and bold'.

Kilspindie Church

Harry tells the story of the Barns of Ayr which happened about this time. Scots lords were invited to talks at the Barns, and as soon as they entered unarmed, they were hung by the English troops – 'where eighteen score were hanged by Saxon seed'. Wallace heard the news of this and grieved for the injuries being perpetrated against his countrymen. (It is this atrocity which forms the opening scenes in the film *Braveheart*.)

Harry describes Wallace's first retaliation against the occupying English forces whilst he was in Dundee. (MAP A15) He was walking through the town when he was approached by young Selbie, son of the English constable of Dundee. Wallace was wearing a suit of green, and Selbie, who was aged about twenty, confronted him, asking why a Scot should be allowed to wear such fine clothes. He then reached for the knife hanging from Wallace's belt. Wallace, already an extremely powerful individual, grabbed Selbie by the throat, and stabbed him to death. He then sprinted away, pursued by Selbie's entourage.

The site of this incident is marked today by a little-known plaque, inserted in the wall to the left of the steps which lead up to the front door of St Paul's Episcopal Cathedral in the High Street. It is worded as follows:

Site of Castle of Dundee
Destroyed circa 1314. Near this spot William Wallace
struck the first blow for Scottish Independence circa 1288.

Tradition has it that the incident took place here, in the vicinity of the castle. Nearby Castle Street is a pointer to this

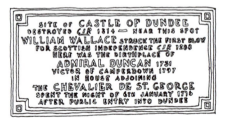

Wallace Plaque, Dundee

being the site of the castle. The reason the plaque mentions that the castle was destroyed in 1314, is because Robert the Bruce's policy was to destroy such strongholds, since the English could not control the country if there were no strongholds for their garrisons to occupy.

Wallace is said to have escaped Selbie's men by running into an inn where he was known. The quick-thinking landlady dressed him in a gown and set him to work at a spinning wheel, and the soldiers passed him by, without realising how close their quarry was. The stone on which Wallace supposedly sat whilst spinning was kept and handed down through the generations, and is now in the McManus Galleries in Dundee.

After Wallace escaped from Dundee, he made contact with his mother at Kilspindie, where she decided the best course of action was for them to dress as pilgrims and head for the shrine of St Margaret at Dunfermline. Harry states that they took the ferry over the Tay to Lindores, where the ruins of a once great abbey still stand. From there they walked through the Ochil Hills to Dunfermline. St Margaret's tomb and shrine lie outside the eastern end of Dunfermline Abbey, but her remains are no longer there. Her head had been a venerated relic, but was last seen at the Scots College at Douai in northern France from which it disappeared during the French revolution. Other relics of St Margaret are apparently to be found at the Escorial near Madrid.

After spending a night at Dunfermline, Wallace and his mother crossed the Forth and went to Linlithgow, then made their way to Dunipace where they stayed with a priest who was a relative. Tradition states that this man, who may have been an uncle of Wallace's, taught him these lines:

Freedom is best, I tell thee true,
Of all things to be won,
then never live within the bonds of slavery, my son.

Wallace evidently spent much time at Dunipace, which stood on the edge of the vast Torwood. (MAP B31) This forest covered much of the area between Falkirk and Stirling, and the Forth and the Campsies, in the late 1200s. Wallace used this woodland to great effect in later life, and he probably got to know its paths and hidden places while staying at Dunipace during his youth.

It is still possible to visit the remains of the church that Wallace knew at Dunipace. In Wallace's time, the town now known as Dunipace was called the Mill of Dunipace and was further up the River Carron from Dunipace proper. The name is a corruption of Duin-na-Bais, gaelic for 'hills of death'. These hills gave their name to the whole parish, including modern Dunipace, and stand just to the east of the M876 where it crosses the Carron. Originally there were three hills, but one was dug away in the 1830s. Although the surviving two look man-made, they are the result of deposits from the last ice age. This is consecrated ground and known as 'the hills of Dunipace cemetery'. When you enter the cemetery, there are ancient yew trees and a low wall to one side. Among these are some old tombstones which date back to the 1600s, and the scant remains of stonework. I have sat on top of the symmetrical hill above these remains, as Wallace must have done when he stayed at Dunipace, and looked out over the River Carron. It is said that the Roman Emperor, Severus, concluded a peace here with the Caledonians. Edward of England certainly visited the spot, because he signed a warrant dated 14 October, 1301, at Dunipace. It is also said to have been on this spot that Wallace confronted Bruce after the Battle of Falkirk, and opened his eyes to the reality of the state of his country.

Wallace and his mother left Dunipace and made their way

back to Elderslie, where his mother's brother told them the terrible news that Wallace's father had been killed by the English. Blind Harry states that his elder brother, Malcolm, had been killed too, but we know that Malcolm outlived Wallace, so unless there was another brother we do not know about, Harry was mistaken in this instance.

At this point in Harry's narrative, Wallace's mother decided to live quietly at Elderslie, while Wallace moved on to stay at Riccarton, another Wallace family property. It was while staying here that he became embroiled in another melee with English soldiers. He was fishing in Irvine Water (MAP B16) when he was approached by five soldiers from the retinue of Lord Percy, one of whom demanded Wallace's catch. Wallace replied that he was willing to hand over half of it. The Englishman demanded it all, and drew his sword. Wallace felled him with his fishing rod and grabbed the sword. He killed three of the five men, and the other two escaped. Harry tells how, when Percy heard the news that one Scot had bettered five of his troops, he said that he would not look for retribution against one man who could hold his own against five English blades. After the incident Wallace had to leave Riccarton as he was now a marked man.

This escapade is supposed to have taken place where the Kilmarnock Water enters the River Irvine, a little west of Riccarton. An inn called the Bickering Bush stood close by until recently, but was demolished to make way for the A71 road from Kilmarnock to Irvine. The name of the inn was said to derive from the incident, and its sign was of men fighting. A footpath leads to the junction of the two rivers. The area is increasingly under development.

When talking of Wallace's early days, we must include Paisley Abbey in any conjecture. (MAP B21) The Abbey stands in the centre of Paisley, on the banks of the River Cart. As the second son of a prominent local

landowner, there is a possibility that Wallace would have received some sort of early education at the Abbey. When you walk through the cloisters to enter Paisley

Paisley Abbey

Abbey, the old doorway on the left is a Norman archway, and was the entrance in Wallace's day. So, if he was schooled here, or even attended services with his parents or family, he would have entered the Abbey through this doorway.

It was said to be at Paisley that his love for the psalms was instilled. It is recorded that at his execution at Smithfield in London, Wallace, as a condemned man, requested that the psalter be held open before his darkening eyes 'til they had done all that they would with him'. Wallace, as a second son, may have been destined to be trained as a priest. Second sons were often enrolled in the priesthood since the elder brother would be expected to inherit the father's propert. Whatever the case, events overtook what might originally have been planned for Wallace's future.

The Wallace Memorial Window in Paisley Abbey was erected in 1873 and depicts Wallace as Samson, after a conflict, giving thanks to God. The window was made by James Ballantyne and Son of Edinburgh, and has the following inscription:

To the Memory of the Knight of Elderslie in this parish. Erected by the Glasgow St Andrew's Society.

The base of the design contains the shield of Wallace wreathed with the Scottish thistle and supported by swords, upon a groundwork of the St Andrew's Cross. In the upper arched part of the window is an ascending angel, emblematical of freedom rendering asunder the chains and shackles of bondage.

It is worth mentioning that Robert III, King of Scots, is buried at Paisley Abbey, as is Marjory, daughter of Robert the Bruce, and all the high Stewards of Scotland, including James who was Steward in Wallace's day.

Wallace Window, Paisley

After the fight at Irvine Water, Wallace is next described by Blind Harry hiding out in Leglen Wood. By tradition, Wallace had a relative who owned the lands of Auchencruive on the River Ayr, where Auchencruive Agricultural College stands today, just outside Ayr on the Mauchline road. (MAP B6) When you travel down the road through the College and come to the old bridge known as Oswald's Bridge, the wooded banks are the remains of Leglen Wood. On the right just after crossing the bridge stands a huge cairn among the trees. This cairn was erected in memory of both Wallace and Robert Burns. Burns as a boy had read the works of Blind Harry and they had a profound effect on him. He would later state, 'The story of Wallace poured a Scottish

Leglen Wood Cairn

prejudice into my veins, which will boil along until the floodgates of life shut in eternal rest.' Burns also wrote of his admiration for Wallace in a letter to a Mrs Dunlop dated 15 November, 1786:

> I chose a fine summer Sunday, the only day of the week in my power and walked half a dozen miles to pay my respects to 'the Leglen Wood' with as much devout enthusiasm as ever pilgrim did to Lorreto; and as I explored every den and dell where I supposed my heroic countryman might have sheltered, I recollect (for even then I was a rhymer) that my heart glowed with a wish to be able to make a song on him equal to his merits.

Just such a song was written by Burns, who composed the stirring words of *Scots wha hae* to the tune of an ancient marching song from the time of the Wars of Independence.

While lurking in Leglen Wood, Harry describes Wallace making forays into the town of Ayr, which was the base for a large English garrison. (MAP B5) On the first of these visits, Wallace came across a giant Englishman offering to let passers-by strike him across the back with a large pole for a groat (4 pennies). Wallace took up this offer, and broke the unfortunate showman's spine, then had to draw his sword to fight his way clear through the English soldiers who had gathered around.

On Wallace's second visit to the town, he was carrying a basket of fish, which was demanded from him by the Steward of Lord Percy. Wallace declined to hand over his basket, whereupon the Englishman struck him with his staff. Like the earlier incident in Dundee, Wallace grasped his assailant by the throat, pulled his dagger, and stabbed him to death. But this time Wallace was surrounded and dragged off to the dungeons of the tolbooth to await trial.

The tollbooth in Ayr at that time stood in the High Street, and when it was demolished, a house was erected on the spot. This house, which in turn was demolished many years ago, had a carved head on the front which locals pointed to as a likeness of Wallace.

Other memorials to Wallace survive in Ayr. 'The Wee Wallace' is a statue in a niche at first floor level in a building on the corner of Newmarket Street and High Street. When Newmarket Street was being surfaced in 1870, two coins were found side by side, one from the reign of Alexander III and one from that of Edward I of England. I am fortunate to have them in my possession.

On the corner of High Street and Mill Vennel is a building known as Wallace's Tower. This was originally a small baronial tower which the council purchased from the Cathcarts of Corbieston in 1673. It was partly reconstructed in 1731, then given a full facelift in the Gothic style in 1834. It now stands 113ft high. Although one of the best known buildings in the town, any real link with Wallace is unknown. Perhaps it was given its name because there is a statue of Wallace on the front, carved by the sculptor Thom.

The two statues of Wallace in Ayr depict a man much older than Wallace. Many statues of Wallace date from Victorian times, when he was made to look middle-aged instead of in his early twenties, probably to give him gravitas.

Wallace languished in the tolbooth, where he had been badly treated and had contracted dysentery. When the jailer came to take him for sentencing, he found him apparently dead, and had him thrown over the wall. The news of this eventually reached the woman who nursed Wallace as a child; she collected his body and it was carried to her house in the New Town of Ayr – that is, the part of Ayr which stands north of the river. She detected a flicker of life, and nursed him back to health. There are echoes in this story of the Resurrection.

Many of these tales are, of course, apocryphal, but we have no other source but Blind Harry for any account of Wallace's early days. It must be stated though, that Harry claims in his poem that he used the works of John Blair as source material. John Blair is thought to have been Wallace's personal chaplain, the story being that they had met up at school in Dundee. Blair fought beside Wallace in most of his campaigns. After Wallace was murdered, Blair, encouraged by Bishop Sinclair of Dunkeld (who we certainly know existed), wrote a biography of Wallace's life and times. It is thought that Bishop Sinclair may have intended to try to have Wallace canonised, and had the book commissioned to send to the Pope. Harry mentions that he had access to Blair's work, but all trace of it has disappeared. What a find this book would be – a first-hand account of the life of Wallace. It has been speculated that there may be a copy in the Vatican archives, lost among many millions of documents. Although all inquiries so far have drawn a blank, the hope still remains that it may one day turn up.

At the time of Wallace's recovery from his sojourn in Ayr tolbooth, Thomas the Rhymer is said to have made a prophecy regarding his future. Thomas the Rhymer, also known as True Thomas, was in reality Thomas of Ercildoune. Legend has it that he was kidnapped by the queen of Elfland, and when he came back from Elfland via a cave in the Eildon Hills, he had the gift of prophecy. What he prophesised was as follows:

Before that Wallace die
Out of this land he shall the Southron send,
And thousands on the field make their last end,
He Scotland thrice shall bring into great peace
And Southron aye be frightened at his face.

This Scottish Nostradamus also predicted the death of Alexander III. Certainly, from this time on, Wallace was to move from personal brawls to something more organised and far more substantial.

CHAPTER 5

Edward I of England – 'Longshanks'

NOT A SINGLE SPEARMAN who followed Wallace into battle is known by name, but these were men moved by patriotic fervour to rid their land of an unwanted oppressor.

Edward's army was another matter altogether. His men followed orders which resulted from his own aggressive ambition with regard to Scotland. Obviously propaganda would have influenced his troops; for example, a story was spread that Wallace had organised choirs of naked Englishmen and Englishwomen to sing for him, then tortured them. But the attitude that prevailed stemmed from Edward himself, not from a collective defensive policy, as it did on the Scottish side.

Edward was well into his fifties when his ambitions regarding Scotland came to the fore. His character was shaped by his earlier years and the major events that took place during his reign.

Edward was the eldest child of Henry III of England and Eleanor of Provence. He was born at Westminster in London on the night of 17 June, 1239, and was baptised in Westminster Abbey.

From an early age he was noted for his outbursts of temper. The chronicler, Matthew Paris, described an unwarranted attack by Edward and some of his friends on a young man: they cut off one of the man's ears and gouged out an eye.

Edward was also unreliable. He would promise one thing then do another, whenever he could see something to gain from a situation. This was not altogether a bad thing, of course, for the king of a country like England at that time would need a certain amount of aggression and deviousness. But Edward's outbursts were uncontrolled, often against members of his own family.

He was fond of falconry, kept his own birds, and was an excellent horseman. He excelled at jousting, practising endlessly at the lists, and throughout his life there are mentions of various injuries he sustained while taking part in tournaments. His bravery has certainly never been doubted.

We know some details of his appearance. He was a long-legged individual, hence his nickname 'Longshanks'. He was tall for the times he lived in, although not the near 7ft that some chroniclers claimed, for when his tomb was opened in 1774, his skeleton was found to be 6ft 2ins tall. He had blond hair that eventually turned white, and he was always depicted as being clean shaven. Most sources mention that he had a drooping eyelid.

At the opening of his tomb (in the presence of the Dean of Westminster and a number of antiquarians), the lid was easily removed as it was not cemented into place. Inside was a marble coffin, in which his body was found to be remarkably well preserved, much of the flesh intact. He was dressed in a red silk tunic and elaborate stole, his lower half covered in cloth of gold. He carried a sceptre surmounted with a cross in his right hand, and another surmounted with a dove in his left. On his head was an open crown. There was no trace of a beard. Before his tomb was closed it was noticed that one of his fingers was missing. One of the antiquarians had stolen it!

Edward was married at the age of fifteen to Eleanor of Castile who was ten. She was to bear him sixteen children.

Edward spent much of his life ravaging others' lands, or taking part in skirmishes. He only fought three full-scale battles. Two of these took place in England while he was still a young man. Simon de Montford had rebelled against his father, Henry III, and Edward led a wing of his father's army at the Battle of Lewes, near Brighton, in 1264. Although the royal forces were finally defeated, Edward's division fought with honour. The rebellion was finally quashed at the Battle of Evesham, where the royalist troops were victorious and de Montford was killed. The third battle that Edward fought was against Wallace at Falkirk.

Edward was also a crusader. In August 1270 he set sail with many other knights to prove himself against the infidel. On the crusade he had the first of the many lucky escapes from death that punctuated his life. He based himself at Acre, which was often used as a starting point by crusaders, and was besieged by the forces of Sultan Baybars. Edward knew that he did not have the manpower to oppose such a large army, but luckily Baybars left and headed for Egypt.

The following is an account of the attempt on Edward's life by a Templar of Tyre:

A Saracen man-at-arms came to Acre to be baptised. Edward had him christened, and took him into his household. This man established himself as a servant to Prince Edward, one who would go and spy out the Saracens and discover where they were vulnerable. One night, the Saracen went to the bedroom where Edward and his wife were sleeping, he took the interpreter with him, and made out that he had just come back from a spying trip and wanted to speak to Edward. The Prince opened the door himself, wearing only his shirt and drawers. The Saracen went up to him and struck a knife in his hip, making a deep and dangerous wound. Edward felt the blow and he hit the man on the temple with his fist, which knocked him senseless to the floor for the moment, then the Prince picked up a table-knife which was in the room and struck the man on the head and killed him. The alarm was raised among his attendants who saw their lord was hurt and roused the whole of Acre. The lords came to the wounded Prince and sent for all the physicians and slaves, who sucked the wound and drew out the poison, so that he made a good recovery, thanks be to God. Edward left the Holy Land on 22nd September 1272 and crossed the sea to return to England.

Although Edward's crusade was not a resounding success, it did at least give him stature among his peers. While he was at Acre his father died, and he returned home to be crowned King. The coronation took place in August 1274.

Edward then began the complete annexation of Wales, building the mighty castles that still dot its landscape. It was made into a new principality, and when his son, later to be Edward II, was born in the new fortress at Caernarfon, he was created the first Prince of Wales. Since that time the heir to the throne of England has always borne the title Prince of Wales.

Alexander's death at Kinghorn opened the door for Edward's aggression towards Scotland, and his run of luck continued. Two months before the Battle of Stirling Bridge,

Edward's horse plunged over the sea defences at Winchelsea but Edward managed to control it with superb horsemanship. In 1304, at the siege of Stirling Castle, a Scot on the battlements fired a crossbow bolt which went through Edward's clothing and lodged in his saddle, leaving him unharmed. During the same siege, a stone fired from the castle actually dropped the horse beneath him, but again Edward walked away unhurt.

An account in the annals of Waverley Abbey in 1291 say that Edward announced to his magnates and councillors that he intended to bring Scotland under his control, as he had Wales. This goes against various English writers who stated that all he wished to do was choose the correct ruler after Alexander's untimely death, and it brings suspicion on his conduct all through the time of the competition for the throne of Scotland. Certainly, later chroniclers in Scotland saw Edward as a demon in human form.

The Scotichronicon, written in the 1440s, states:

> This King Edward is said to have been the thirteenth in succession from that Geoffrey count of Anjou, who married a she-devil dressed in human form. It was from their seed that Edward was descended. Indeed he has been likened to the backside of a weathercock and the tailend of all the dregs of his devilish race. Similarly it has been foretold by a certain man that that devilish race would in no way be redeemed until the thirteenth generation.

Edward was responsible for many reforms in government in England, and is seen as a strong, if at times wilful, ruler. In Scotland though, he is remembered in a completely different light. It was his command that led to the horrific slaughter at Berwick. It was on his orders that Dunfermline Abbey was burnt after he had wintered there in 1304, even though it contained his sister's tomb. It was he who had Wallace murdered, though he was the noblest enemy Edward ever had. He had spared many others, some of whom were not fit to be mentioned in the same sentence as Wallace. And it was his personal ambition alone that started the war between two previously peaceful countries, the legacy of which is with us still.

However, there is one redeeming factor for me, as a Scot, in all of this – he did not win.

CHAPTER 6

A More Concerted Effort

WALLACE'S FIRST ATTACK AS commander of a group of like-minded young men, according to Blind Harry, took place at Loudoun Hill on the road to Ayr.

Wallace had heard that an English baggage-train would be travelling along the road between Lanark and Ayr, going via Strathaven and then over the moor to the infant River Irvine, under Loudoun Hill. From here the route continued downriver to the Kilmarnock area, then swung south for Ayr. Wallace was determined that the English supplies would get no further than Loudoun Hill, where he planned an ambush.

Loudoun Hill

This hill is a conspicuous conical summit, the remains of an extinct volcano, and is said to be the greatest defensive site in all southern Scotland. Its name is made up from the Scots-Irish 'Dun' and the Scots-Saxon 'Law', to form Law-Dun-Hill or 'hill-hill-hill'. Its summit has been the site of various Roman and Pictish fortifications over the centuries. (MAP B15)

Wallace had apparently learned that the commander of this baggage train was a knight by the name of Fenwick, who legend says was responsible for the murder of Wallace's father. Harry has Wallace telling his men 'Here was my father slain'. If this was the case, it must have been sweet revenge indeed for Wallace to confront Fenwick at the spot where his father met his end.

His companions on this occasion were said to include his eighteen-years-old cousin, Adam Wallace, the heir to Riccarton, his nephew Edward Little, Cleland, another relation, and Robert Boyd from the Kilmarnock district. Boyd was a famous name in the area, the family having been granted land there after the Battle of Largs.

We can imagine the skirmish that took place on the road under Loudoun Hill. No doubt boulders would have been prised out of the ground to be hurled at the English baggage-horses far below. Wallace's men mounted a ferocious attack, with Wallace dispatching Fenwick himself, and the others routing the English men at arms.

Large scale maps show that a small hummock above the River Irvine on the east of Loudoun Hill is named Wallace's Knowe. Whether this is where the fight took place or possibly where Wallace's father died is not known, but the name has survived.

More intriguing is Wallace's Cairn, which stood near the A71 road, where there is now a sand quarry. Although the cairn is no longer there, it is still shown on quite recent maps, and with large scale maps it is easy to pinpoint its exact site, using as axis the old railway bridges that still stand on the other side of the road. This shows that the cairn stood just a few yards in from the edge of the quarry. When I was trying to find out why the pile of stones had been called Wallace's

Cairn, in the early 1990s I spoke to an elderly woman who lived on a nearby farm. She could recall going to the kirk in nearby Darvel by horse and cart with her father, and he would often point out the stones to her, stating that they marked the site where Wallace buried the English dead. When the sand quarry started to develop, she remembered asking her father, 'What about Wallace's stones?' He told her not to worry as they would never be touched, but unfortunately he was wrong. One day as they were passing they saw that the quarry had been expanded over the area where the stones had stood.

I have often wondered if anything might have been found under these stones, and have looked in vain for an old photograph of the cairn. The stones may mark the site of the slain who proved luckier than the soldiers Wallace captured. It is said that they were forced to carry the spoils to Clyde's Wood, where he hung them out of hand.

The village of Coalburn near Lesmahagow has a Wallace's Cave said to be Wallace's base when he was in this area. Where Coalburn stands today was once part of Clyde's Wood, so there may be a connection. The cave has deteriorated vastly, partly from collapse but mostly from being in the middle of open-cast mining operations. A visitor to the site in 1997 said there was no point in even taking a photograph of the site. (MAP B14)

After Loudoun Hill, Wallace's reputation was beginning to spread. His next attack was on a 'peel', or fortification, at Gargunnock, west of Stirling, which had been built and garrisoned to command a ford across the River Forth. (MAP B28) Wallace and his men are said to have taken up position on nearby Keir Hill, and when the time was ripe, attacked and routed the garrison. The fortification comprised a central keep, surrounded by a wooden palisade. It stood about 150 feet from the Forth, about a mile north-east of the village. Although there is now no trace of the site, some of the ditch surrounding it could still be seen in the 1800s. The site should not be confused with Gargunnock House, the core of which is a tower house of a later date than Wallace's time.

At the raid on Gargunnock Wallace was joined by many new recruits, including an Irishman called Stephen, and a surly individual by the name of Faudon.

After holding the peel for four days, on the fifth they marched north, crossing the River Teith and then the Earn, and made their way to St John's Town of Perth. (MAP A12)

Although Perth is an ancient town, very little that is recognisable from Wallace's time has survived. The Church of St John (who gave the town its original name) stands in the town centre, and has seen many changes over the centuries. The town lades, or mill streams, survive and were in existence long before Wallace. Walls of sufficient strength to resist vigorous sieges surrounded the town from a very early date until the later 18th century. The old castle of Perth stood outside the walls, at the end of the Skinnergate, but it has completely disappeared.

Wallace and his followers made a surprise attack on the castle, but the alarm was raised and a scuffle took place during which Wallace slew the captain of the garrison. The Scots withdrew to Short-Wood Shaws ('shaw' being the old Scots for a tract of woodland) on the Tay north of Perth, where they were besieged by the main English garrison, led by Sir John Butler. A fierce fight ensued, and according to Harry, Wallace slew Butler.

Again and again Harry describes Wallace personally slaying the enemy leader. There may well be some truth in this, as Wallace would know that the ordinary English men-at-arms would be less willing to continue the fight if their leader was dead. It is easy to imagine Wallace in the thick of the fray, fighting through the press to attack the enemy commander, swinging his two-handed sword, blood lust evident on his face, driven on by the fire of passion for the freedom of his country.

Wallace had a lover in Perth, and the English, knowing of her association with him, had bribed her to inform them of his next visit, but when Wallace arrived, she told him of this, and he disguised himself in female garb to slip away. However, two guards on the town's South Inch were suspicious 'at such a sturdy queen'. They questioned Wallace, and he pulled his sword and killed them both. He then hurried to join his band before the alarm was raised.

The bodies of the guards were eventually discovered, and the garrison set out in force, to capture or kill Wallace. They found him and his men, and a running battle ensued, the Scots heavily outnumbered. As they ran, the English kept hot on their trail by using a bloodhound. Faudon constantly slowed the Scots down, complaining of tiredness. Wallace urged him on, but as Faudon continued to hold the Scots up, he eventually smelled a rat, realising that Faudon was slowing them up on purpose. Wallace drew his sword in fury and with one mighty swing, parted Faudon's head from his shoulders. He then explained the situation to his men, saying that Faudon has not died uselessly, as his blood would confuse the dog.

The incident took place in a small wood at Dupplin, about five miles south-west of Perth, and Stephen, Wallace's faithful Irish companion, and Kerlie, one of his most loyal followers, elected to stay behind and hide near Faudon's body to try to create confusion when their pursuers caught up. The bloodhound, of course, went straight to the headless body, and as the English troops gathered round, Stephen and Kerlie stabbed the commander, Sir Gerard Heron, in the back. In the gloom of the woods, they made good their escape.

Wallace was worried about his friends, and decided to go back and try to find them. He camped that night in the Gask area. Gask stands a little north of the A9 between Auchterarder and Perth.

At this point in Blind Harry's tale, he describes a strange nightmare-like sequence where Wallace was confronted by Faudon's blood-spattered ghost, holding his head aloft in his right hand. Wallace fled from this apparition, covering endless miles, until eventually he reached the River Forth, where he plunged into its icy waters. He was found on the far side of the river, faint and delirious, by a woman who recognised him. She took him home, and with strong sons to guard the house, nursed Wallace back to health. There may be some truth behind this part of Harry's tale, for with Wallace constantly on the move, often sleeping under the stars, and always living life on a knife's edge, he may have started to break down under the strain, suffering the equivalent of shell-shock.

On his sick bed, he was chided by a priest, who said that he should quit the fight and accept Edward of England as his lord. Wallace pointed out the wrongs that Scotland was suffering and made it clear that his sword was keen and thirsty for blood, at which point the door opened to reveal Stephen and Kerlie, and tears were shed at their reunion. They told Wallace how they had slain Sir Gerard Heron as he leaned over Faudon's body. This news gave Wallace the medicine he needed to regain his strength, and he and his band set off, accompanied by the sons of the woman who had nursed him back to health. Following the River Carron up into the Campsie Hills, they made their way to Dundaff.

Dundaff Castle was the home of an aged knight named Sir John de Graham. He was a true patriot, but too old to live the life that Wallace and his band had carved out. But his son, Sir John the Younger, joined Wallace and became one of his most trusted companions. It is possible that Wallace and Sir John had met earlier, when Wallace was staying with his uncle, the priest at Dunipace, several miles downstream from Dundaff.

The earthworks of Dundaff Castle are still clearly visible, and stand a few hundred yards north of the dam at the western end of the Carron Valley Reservoir. The source of the river Carron lies under the reservoir, and the castle was built to command the fertile site. A forestry road opposite the dam branches north off the B818, and takes you up to the castle site which is an idyllic place to be on a summer's day. (MAP B27) The castle moat dates from earliest times, but the traces of stonework are of a building of a later date.

From here Wallace set off again, going south to Clydesdale, and halted at Kirkfieldbank, below Lanark. (MAP B13) It is at this point that Blind Harry mentions Wallace's love, who legend says was Marion Braidfute, the heiress of Lamington near Lanark. Wallace supposedly first saw her in St Kentigern's Church in Lanark. The remains of this church stand in the cemetery to the south-west of the town, and date from the early 1200s. Legend has it that Wallace and Marion married here. The original St Kentigern's was reported as being in a ruinous condition by 1637, and was replaced by the new building in 1777. Its bell was transferred to the new

St Kentigerns Church,
Lanark

church according to the inscription on it, which states that it
has 'three times, Phenix-like, past thro' fiery furnace', in
1110, 1659 and 1740. If this is the case, Wallace would have
been familiar with the sound of the original bell. (MAP B12)

Harry's story continues, with Wallace's band journeying
south to Lochmaben, where they managed to draw the
garrison out of the castle by stratagem. Sir John de Graham
slew Graystock, the enemy commander, and the Scots took
the castle, although Blair, Wallace's chaplain, was wounded.
The castle was not the large stone fortress by the loch that
most people assume – this site was chosen by Edward of
England after his victory at Falkirk, to consolidate his hold
on Scotland. The castle in Wallace's day stood on the mound,
200ft across and 20ft high, at the side of the Lochmaben golf
course. (MAP B2)

As Wallace and his men returned north, heading for
Lanark, they came to Crawford Castle, where they heard a
drunken party in full swing. The Scots took full advantage of
the situation and launched a surprise attack. De Graham
threw a blazing brand onto the wooden rafters, and the place
was soon on fire.

The remains of this castle, also known as Tower Lindsay,

stand on the opposite bank of the Clyde from the village of Crawford which lies beside the M74 motorway. (MAP B8)

Back in Lanark, Wallace was reunited with Marion whose father had a town house there, and Wallace was apparently welcomed into the household. (MAP B12) The site of this house is marked by a small stone wall with a plaque inserted in it which reads:

> Here stood the house of William Wallace
> Who in Lanark in 1297, first drew
> Sword to free his native land.

The plaque is on the left at the bottom of the High Street, at the top of the Castlegate, just to the side of the parish church. A statue of Wallace stands above the doorway. It was carved in 1817 by a young sculptor, Robert Forrest, and shows Wallace as a middle-aged man, rather than a young man in his twenties.

Site of Wallace House, Lanark

What sparked the violence that followed in Lanark is open to debate, but the generally accepted story is that some soldiers started to taunt Wallace, which he managed to take with good humour, but when a foul jest was made about Marion, his wife, Wallace drew his great sword, and cut off the offender's hand. All hell broke loose, and Wallace ran off down the street to Marion's family home, pursued by soldiers. The door of the house was opened by Marion, and

Wallace ran through and out into the open country beyond. He made his way to a hide-out in a cave on the Cartland Crags above the Mouse Water. Heselrig, the English sheriff, was enraged at Wallace's escape, and in retribution had Marion put to death. Wallace's friends had the unenviable task of informing him of this. We can only imagine the effect the news had on him, but he was about to multiply his efforts for the liberation of his country tenfold.

Lamington Tower

Lamington, of which Marion was the heiress, stands on the Clyde, twelve miles upstream from Lanark, not far from the M74 at Abington. (MAP B9) The remains of the castle lie north of the village, between it and the river. Trees have been planted around the ruins which makes them difficult to spot from a distance. However, access is relatively easy by a track from the nearby farm. The remains are mostly of a tower house, dating from the 15th century, standing on the site of the earlier stronghold. The landscape will have changed little since Wallace's day, and he and Marion must have looked over the river to Tinto, a view very much the same today as then.

Marion is said to have born Wallace a daughter who married Sir William Baillie of Hoprig. Certainly, the Baillies inherited Lamington around this time. The castle and estate then passed down through succeeding generations of Baillies, and the family built a mansion nearby called Lamington House. The old castle still stood in a good state of preservation until it was demolished in 1780 to be used as building material by an ignorant factor.

The little church in Lamington lies in a circular graveyard. (The early Christians would sometimes build their churches on a prehistoric site or the site of an old stone circle to supersede the old religions, forcing them to die out. This may have been the case in Lamington.) On one side of the church is an old Norman archway which would be an entrance in Wallace's day. The doorway has been filled in and has a plaque inserted as a war memorial, but Wallace and Marion may have entered through it to attend church when they were in residence at the castle.

Lamington Church

Over the years I have given consideration to the whereabouts of Marion's grave. Although put to death in Lanark, her body may well have been brought back to the family estate to be interred with her ancestors, so perhaps she lies in the picturesque little churchyard, looking out across the Clyde at Tinto's unchanging features.

Most of the details I have given of Wallace's life so far are conjecture, and the bulk of what I have related comes from the work of Blind Harry. Within months of the incident at Lanark, Wallace was leading an army, which would have been impossible if his was not already a well-kent name.

Although we have no way of proving it, Blind Harry may be closer to the truth than many imagine in his descriptions of the incidents in Wallace's life up to this point. For the next year of his life, along with his final month in 1305, he was suddenly writ large in the history of Scotland.

CHAPTER 7

The Turn of the Tide

IF WE ARE LOOKING AT Wallace's life from the point of view of historical facts, it begins in Lanark in May 1297. A unique little window exists that enables us to see back into the reality of what happened there. The facts were written down in the 1350s, when a Northumbrian knight, Sir Thomas de Grey, from Heaton on the River Till, was imprisoned in Edinburgh Castle. He decided to while away the time by writing a book on the history of the world, and gave prominence to events which happened in his own or his father's lifetime. He tells how, in the month of May 1297, his father was part of the garrison at Lanark when Wallace and his band fell upon the quarters at night, killed the Sheriff and set fire to the place. His father had had good reason to remember, for he was wounded in the fighting and left for dead. Had it not been that he lay between two blazing buildings, he might have died during the chill May night. He was found the next day by a comrade, William de Lundy, and was tended by him until he recovered.

We cannot know if the motive for Wallace's attack on the castle was retribution for Marion's murder, but there is no doubt about his slaying of the English Sheriff whose name was William de Heselrig. He came from Hazelrigg (the modern spelling) in Chatton in Northumberland.

One of the accusations read out at Wallace's trial in 1305 was that he had murdered Heselrig. This is the first incident in which the legend of Wallace becomes hard fact, where the misty man of stories suddenly becomes a real, bloody, avenging angel. Although he is surrounded by a halo of rose-tinted hindsight, Wallace's strength was his determination to slaughter Englishmen wherever and whenever he encountered them. While many were content to live under an oppressor's yoke, merely to live a quiet life, Wallace would accept no shortcuts. He would kill anyone who stood in the way of his country's liberation. But this bogey-man had another side to him, which showed itself later in acts of diplomacy.

Certainly, the many foreign troops based in Scotland must have suddenly considered their own situation and safety when news spread of what had happened at Lanark. Perhaps this was one of the reasons for Edward Longshanks' unequivocal hatred of Wallace – the fact that he would do something as outragious as firing a garrison town and slaughtering its sheriff, that instead of just thinking of doing such things, he had the audacity to carry them out.

The castle at Lanark in Wallace's day stood at the very bottom of the Castlegate which leads down from the left-hand side of the church which bears his statue. At the bottom of the street is a bowling green which stands on top of the earthworks of the once proud fortress. If you walk to the far side of the green and look over the hedge, you can see where the various defences have been on the embankment sloping down from the castle. The road leading up into the bowling club is probably the original castle entrance, and there may have been a drawbridge here at one time. At the entrance to the bowling green is a stone with a small plaque stating that parliaments of Scotland were once held here. It is strange how a place which once witnessed such bloodshed is now the venue for quiet games of bowls on summer's evenings.

Blind Harry has Wallace in battle at Biggar straight after Lanark (MAP B10). There is no record of such a battle taking place, although there may have been some sort of skirmish, and it has been suggested that Harry may have confused this with the Battle of Roslin. Wallace then travels south to make an assault on Cruggleton Castle. Some ruins of this castle remain, on the western shore of Wigton Bay in Galloway close to Whithorn. (MAP B3)

Harry then relates that Wallace went to Rutherglen for a meeting in the church. Although this is conjecture, it is worth noting that the spire of this church still stands in the graveyard immediately west of the town hall in Main Street, the rest of the church having been demolished in 1794. (MAP B24) This church is mentioned by Harry again later in his narrative, for he names it as the place where Sir John Menteith agreed to betray Wallace to the English.

Rutherglen was an important town and port in Wallace's time. It had an impressive castle, a fact probably unknown to most of today's inhabitants. It stood in King Street, close to Castle Street, but was abandoned in the early 1700s. It was extensively used by the locals for building materials until not a trace remained.

Next in Harry's narrative, Wallace is close to Monkton church in Ayrshire when he has a dream. (MAP B7) In this dream, Wallace is approached by a man who gives him a sword of the finest steel and leads him to the top of a high mountain from which he can see Scotland ablaze below. The man tells Wallace he must avenge the wrongs against his country. A woman then appears and hands Wallace a red and green wand, and makes the sign of the saltire on his face with a sapphire. Wallace then goes into Monkton church to ask the priest the meaning of his dream, and is told that the man was St Andrew and the woman the Blessed Virgin, the wand signifying red for battles and green for courage.

This church was still in use in 1837, when it was reported that it was roofed with oak. The roofless ruins stand in Monkton to this day (hard by the runway of Prestwick Airport), and the remaining walls are nearly four feet thick in places.

From Monkton to Ayr is only four miles and it was in Ayr that one of Wallace's most famous escapades took place, although there is no documentary evidence for it. The Barns of Ayr is mentioned earlier as being the site of an atrocity where unarmed and unwary Scots were murdered. Wallace decided to exact revenge. (MAP B5)

There was a large English garrison at Ayr, and as all the troops could not be lodged within the castle, about 500 soldiers were billeted in the timber barns which were probably coated in pitch. Wallace with fifty men stationed a man at each window and door. Combustible material was gathered, probably gorse bushes, and stacked against the woodwork. It was then ignited, and in the breeze blowing from the sea, it quickly became an inferno. The place was in an uproar, as men tried to clamber out through the windows, only to find a Scot with a sword or an axe ready outside. They were either killed on the spot, or pushed back into the burning building.

While this was going on, Wallace had sent Boyd with a small party to keep an eye on the garrison within the castle. The castle stood near the mouth of the River Ayr, close to the modern swimming baths. On the site are some fragments of stonework and a little corner turret, but these are the remains of a later fort built by Cromwell around the site of the former castle.

The site of the Barns of Ayr, however, is open to conjecture. A Roman road ran to Ayr from Dumfriesshire. It traversed the town along the line of what is now Mill Street, and seems to have terminated in either a military station or a harbour at the mouth of the river, where the later castle stood. Old gazetteers say that the Barns stood on the south-east side of the town, on or near the site of Townhead Quarry on the line of the Roman road. There are other claims for where they were sited, one of which is near the south end of the auld brig of Ayr. This is feasible, as the Barns would not have been situated too far from the castle.

Another relic of Ayr from the time of Wallace is the tower of St John the Baptist Church which was the site of a parliament of King Robert the Bruce in 1315.

As Wallace rode inland, away from Ayr, he is said to have halted on a hilltop and looked back and remarked, 'The Barns of Ayr burn well'. There is a hill which bears the name

of Barnweill, which may commemorate the incident, but much earlier charters than those of Wallace's era refer to this hill as Berenbouell of which Barnweill is obviously a corruption, or has been adapted to fit. (MAP B17) Nevertheless, a monument shaped like a small baronial tower was built on the hill in 1855, with plaques telling the story of Wallace. (The keys to the monument are available

Barnweill Tower

in Ayr, and the details are signposted at the monument.) Unfortunately, you cannot see the view towards Ayr that Wallace had from the hill, as a farm now blocks it. Barnweill is visible from the A77, on your left as you pass the turn-off for Craigie, heading south-west towards Ayr. It stands between the villages of Craigie and Tarbolton, and a single track road takes you to within a few yards of the monument.

Next in Blind Harry's tale Wallace makes an attack on Glasgow. Although there is no real evidence to confirm this, an old history of Glasgow has the following entry:

Edward had appointed one of this creatures named Anthony Beck during the captivity of Robert Wishart, Bishop of Glasgow; and a large English force, under Earl Percy, was stationed in the neighbourhood of the cathedral. Wallace left Ayr with his company of 300 and made in hot haste for Glasgow. After crossing Glasgow bridge Wallace divided his followers into two bodies, one of which, led by himself, marched by the High Street, while the other, under the Laird of Auchinleck, 'for he the passage kend' went by St Mungo's Lane and the Drygate. Percy had a force of 1,000 men, and with these between Bell O' the Brae and the site of the old university he met the body under Wallace. While the battle was doubtful the other body came rushing on from the Drygate, Percy being cut down by Wallace himself. The English were seized with a panic, and fled in all directions, notwithstanding that they were 'gud men off wer' like 'all Northummyrland'.

Wallace and his crew then make a sally into the highlands, to deal with traitors there under the command of a man called McFadzean. This McFadzean was apparently working with the blessing of John of Lorne, who throughout the Wars of Independence invariably took Edward Longshanks' side.

Wallace's men marched through Strathfillan to Loch

Dochart, where they apparently rested for a while. The showdown with McFadzean's forces is traditionally said to have taken place in the Pass of Brander at the northern end of Loch Awe, a dark and deep defile, that even today, traversed by a modern road and railway, still has echoes of the times of great battles, overshadowed as it is by mighty Ben Cruachan. (MAP B36) The patriots attacked the traitors here with such vigour that the enemy line quickly broke, and when the enemy begged for mercy, Wallace shouted to his cheering warriors:

> They're our own blood, both man and boy
> Such penitents can any heart destroy?'
> Then ordered all Scotsmen that were found
> To save alive, but foreigners cut down.

A council was then held at Ardchattan Priory on the north shore of Loch Etive, a few miles east of Connel Ferry. (MAP B37) This Priory, dedicated to St Modan, was founded in 1231. All that is left is part of the choir, with a north aisle, a piscina under a tooth-moulded arch, and fragments of piers suggesting a central tower. There is no official record of Wallace having been here, although Robert the Bruce is said to have held a parliament here in 1308, which was the last time Gaelic was the language spoken at a parliament.

Another episode from around this time which we know actually took place, was Wallace's raid on Scone. (MAP A13) Scone was the ancient crowning place of the Kings of Scots, and Edward had stolen the Stone of Destiny from here the year before. It is a place dear to the hearts of Scots, and Wallace's raid would have cheered many. On this escapade he was joined by Sir William Douglas, father of Bruce's faithful companion, the Good Sir James. Backed by a hardy band, they descended on Scone in a lightening raid and surprised the English justiciar, William Ormsby, who was holding court there. Ormsby was lucky to escape, legend stating that he ran for his life with the Scots' swords inches from his back, but he left behind all his baggage and the Scots captured much valuable booty.

This took place at the original Scone, which stood just over a mile from where the village stands today. All that remains of it is the town cross, which is in the grounds of Scone Palace. I have heard of many towns losing their crosses, but this must be the only cross which has lost its town! It is one of the great losses of our history that all the old buildings at Scone have disappeared. The Abbey and Palace were destroyed by a mob in 1559 during the Reformation. There is not even a trace of the tomb of Robert II of Scotland who was buried here. Edifices that had seen hundreds of years of attendances by the mighty, of crownings and coronation ceremonies, even a royal burial, were swept away in a day in the name of reformed religion. There is so much in our historic little land that has been lost. Many priceless wonders that were not destroyed by invading English armies were destroyed by Scots themselves, fired by religious zeal. Scotland is dotted with empty shells that were once furnished and equipped with artefacts from every century, such as Linlithgow Palace, Holyrood Abbey and all the great religious houses of the Borders. Even the tomb of the mighty Bruce at Dunfermline was lost to us. This was a heritage that nothing can replace. All we can do is hope to learn from our past and ensure that such a thing never happens again.

From Scone, Blind Harry next takes Wallace into the north-east, marching through the Mearns to Dunnottar Castle. (MAP A19) The castle was besieged, the English soldiers

Dunnottar Castle

locked themselves within the church to make a last stand, the church was fired, and they all perished. Dunnottar Castle is open to the public and stands on its cliff-girt stack, a little south of Stonehaven.

From here the Scots marched the few miles north to Aberdeen, where Harry describes the harbour as being crammed with English shipping. (MAP A20) Wallace fired the shipping, causing havoc, with many ships sunk and many badly damaged. There is a bronze statue of Wallace in Aberdeen 'returning defiant answer to the English Ambassadors before the Battle of Stirling Bridge'.

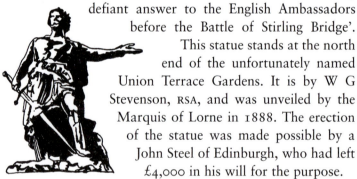

Wallace Statue, Aberdeen

This statue stands at the north end of the unfortunately named Union Terrace Gardens. It is by W G Stevenson, RSA, and was unveiled by the Marquis of Lorne in 1888. The erection of the statue was made possible by a John Steel of Edinburgh, who had left £4,000 in his will for the purpose.

After Aberdeen we find the Scots besieging the Castle of Dundee, where Wallace slew Selby, son of the Governor. (MAP A15)

Around this time, Wallace made contact with Andrew Murray. Andrew had been held captive in the castle at Chester, and managed to escape. It is believed he somehow secured a safe-conduct pass to visit his father, who was being held in London, then eluded his guards, eventually returning to his ancestral lands in the Black Isle near Inverness. He came from illustrious stock. His father was a powerful baron, Sir Andrew Murray of Petty. His uncle was Sir William Murray of Bothwell, known as 'The Rich', who had been responsible for the construction of mighty Bothwell Castle, and looking at the ruins today gives one an idea of just how wealthy this man was. It must have cost an huge amount to build such a fortress. (MAP B25)

In May 1297, young Andrew raised the Standard of Scotland over Avoch Castle, and started his revolt against the occupying forces. This was probably around the time Wallace murdered Hesilrig in Lanark. Avoch Castle stood on Ormonde Hill near the village of Avoch, and a cairn commemorating this 'northern uprising' was built there to mark the 700th anniversary in May 1997. (MAP A21)

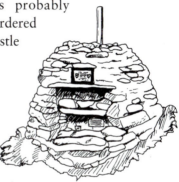

Cairn at Avoch

Things quickly gained momentum, and Murray, aided by the burghers of Inverness under Alexander Pilche, attacked Urquhart Castle on Loch Ness. They then turned east, and in blitzkrieg fashion, cleared the English out of the castles in the northeast.

Wallace, with the army he had gathered in the south, made contact with Murray and his men from the north. They seem to have hit it off right away. Both were prepared to put Scotland's cause before life itself. It would be wonderful to be able to pinpoint the spot where these two young men first came face to face and grasped each other's hand, but legend does not furnish us with this detail.

There was now a multitude of men gathered in Dundee. The news arrived that an English army was marching north to deal with the 'insurrection'. Wallace and Murray knew that this army must cross over Stirling Bridge to reach them. The Forth was too wide further east to be bridged, and the ground was too rough further west, with Flanders Moss ready to sink men and horses, and the edge of the Highlands beyond that. They could not hope to beat the mighty, well-trained and well-horsed English army on an open field, but they might be able to think up some ruse at Stirling. The siege of Dundee Castle was left to Alexander Scrymgeour, aided by the townsfolk, while Murray and Wallace headed south, knowing that the day of reckoning was fast approaching.

CHAPTER 8

Stirling Bridge

WALLACE AND MURRAY ARRIVED in the Stirling area in advance of the English army. One can imagine these two standing on top of the Abbey Craig (a Scots variation of the word crag), looking down at the wooden bridge which spanned the River Forth a mile or so distant from their vantage point. (MAP B30) The Scots soldiers, probably mostly lightly armed spearmen, would have taken up positions around the Abbey Craig, to await developments. The river was approached from the Craig by a causeway over soft ground. The ground was not necessarily marshland or waterlogged, but was probably unsuitable for deploying cavalry because of the weight of armour on both horse and rider. If you stand and look down on the battlesite from the National Wallace Monument, the causeway would not have been too far removed from the line of the road which leads from the Abbey Craig to the river. The cluster of houses at the foot of the Craig bears the name Causewayhead.

Cambuskenneth Abbey

The Abbey Craig takes its name from Cambuskenneth Abbey, the ruins of which lie a little way south at a bend in the river in the village of Cambuskenneth. Wallace was probably familiar with the Abbey, as his uncle, the priest at Dunipace, would most likely have visited the abbey regularly, Dunipace being a dependency of Cambuskenneth. Wallace may have fished in the river, or even climbed to the top of the Craig while his uncle was engaged in church business.

The River Forth is tidal as far as Stirling and has particularly muddy banks. In Wallace's day there would have been rough scrubland above the muddy banks, with some cultivation beyond. The site of the original bridge at Stirling was for many years a matter of debate. Some accounts place the site downstream from Stirling, towards Cambuskenneth, and in contrast to this, an old history of Stirling carries the following:

> A wooden bridge lying north-south across the Forth at Kildean, a point a little west of the longitude of the castle, and about half-a-mile above the old stone bridge, existed at a very early period, and was the scene of the notable exploit of Wallace with the English army. Its site is still a ford, and at low water, exhibits some vestiges of the ancient structure.

The foundations of the bridge in Wallace's and Murray's battle were eventually 're-discovered' in the 1990s, just a little upstream from the later stone bridge. This 'discovery' was widely reported in the press, although locals had informed me of the location prior to this and I have seen references from the early 1900s mentioning this to be the site of the bridge. These foundations, or piers, run across the river at an angle of 45°. This method of construction was probably used to help the structure withstand floods and large debris which could have pulled the whole lot down. Although at the time of writing research has still to be done, it would appear that this bridge rested on eight separate stone piers. It is interesting to note that the ancient seal of the town of Stirling shows a bridge with eight piers supporting it. The bridge stood on the bend of a great loop in the river which almost forms an island on the Abbey Craig side.

The English army arrived in Stirling in the first week of September 1297, having marched north from Berwick. The chronicle of Walter of Guisborough, an English monk, states that this army comprised 1,000 cavalry, with 50,000 foot soldiers, many of them Welsh. We should be sceptical of such numbers, as the same source quotes Wallace's army at 40,000. Although no doubt heavily outnumbered, Wallace and Murray probably had 10,000 men all told.

The English were commanded by John de Warenne, the Earl of Surrey, who had been made Lieutenant or Keeper of Scotland by Edward. He had been in charge of the English at the victory at Dunbar the previous year. He was assisted by Hugh Cressingham, the Treasurer, or as the Scots named him, 'The Treacherer'. He had come to prominence as a steward of the English queen, and even English accounts mention him as being fat and unpopular, with no reputation for honesty.

Several Scots lords met the English leadership at Stirling, among them James the Steward, and Malcolm, Earl of Lennox. As mentioned earlier, the Wallaces were vassals of the Stewards, so technically James was Wallace's feudal superior. The Steward and Lennox said that if they were given a little time they might be able to settle the matter, and sort out the situation without any fighting taking place. As we well know, Wallace and Murray would be very unlikely to take part in any negotiations, and it may have been the case that stalling tactics were being deployed. Certainly the Steward and Lennox returned on 10 September with no change to report, but they then rode off again saying they would return with 40 armed horsemen. Lennox then came across some English foraging; exactly what they were doing has not come down to us, but it upset Lennox enough for the matter to result in bloodshed, one of the English soldiers being slain. At dawn the next day, 11 September, the English horsemen started to cross the bridge. Its narrowness caused them to ride no more than two abreast. But they were recalled since Warenne was still asleep. When he awoke, they were ordered to advance again across the bridge, but were again recalled when the Steward and Lennox were spotted riding toward the English camp, the English believing that they would bring news of a Scottish submission. In fact, they had come to report that they could not talk any Scots into defecting from Wallace and Murray. It would seem obvious to us now that these two noblemen would be relaying information on the strength of the English. As a last resort, Warenne sent two Dominican friars to the Scots to ask them to surrender. Guisborough's chronicle records Wallace's reply:

> Tell your commander that we are not here to make peace but to do battle to defend ourselves and liberate our kingdom. Let them come on, and we shall prove this in their very beards.

Although we have no way of knowing that Wallace actually uttered these words, from what we know of him, it is certainly possible. Friars were the news carriers of their day, having the safe-conduct of their religious habit to be able to move freely around the country, so perhaps this is a true record of what was said. If so, these are the first words uttered by Wallace that have come down to us.

We can picture Wallace and Murray on the Abbey Craig, watching the English cross the bridge several times only to be recalled. The Scots spearmen would also be watching, adrenalin starting to flow in readiness for the forthcoming engagement.

When the Dominican friars returned, Warenne gave the order for a full advance. Sir Richard Lundie asked leave of the English leadership to take a squadron of horse and foot to cross the river upstream at the Fords of Drip, to safeguard the crossing by threatening the Scots' rear. But Cressingham the Treasurer overrode this request, saying that enough of King Edward's money had been squandered, and that battle should be joined immediately. It was to prove much more costly than Cressingham could have imagined.

Legend says that Wallace had a man hidden under the bridge in a basket-style contraption, ready to pull out a dowel, or pin, thereby causing the structure to collapse under the weight of armoured men and horses. According to Blind Harry:

> A cunning carpenter, by name John Wright
> He quickly calls, and falls to work on sight
> Caus'd saw the boards immediately in two
> By the mid trest, that none might over go
> On cornal bands caus'd nail it very soon
> Then fill'd with clay as nothing had been done.

Strange as it may seem, the Wright family owned land at the north end of Stirling Bridge, whether from time immemorial, or in gratitude for this deed, we do not know. The first-born son was always nicknamed Pin in remembrance of the feat, and the last Pin Wright died around the beginning of the 20th century. The family's coat of arms was a carpenter's axe, the crest being a mailed arm grasping an axe.

Harry puts the number of invaders at the 50,000 mark, saying Wallace and Murray were outnumbered six to one. The Scots had to stand patiently as the enemy deployed out from the bridge-end, their heavy cavalry more or less confined to the causeway. We can imagine their eyes darting from the task ahead across to Wallace and Murray, watching for the signal. These men obviously believed in the entity of Scotland, and for once that belief was to be backed by the leadership, who could trust them in return. Every one was there to fight, not for land or riches, but for freedom, and if their life was part of the cost, then so be it.

When he had judged that the numbers who had crossed the bridge were as many as his men could deal with, Wallace blew long and hard on his horn. If we listen hard, we can hear its reverberations echo back from the surrounding hills – but only for a few seconds, as the roar from several thousand Scots throats drowned it out. It was at this moment Pin Wright did what was required of him, and the centre of the bridge collapsed into the river, men and horses plunging in. The Scots sprinted towards the bridge in a scissors manoeuvre, both sides reaching the bridge-end simultaneously, thereby cutting off those north of the river from their comrades on the south side. This part of the English army was now trapped in the great U-bend of the river, and the bulk of the Scots began closing in, their spear points levelled. The heavy cavalry, so devastating in an organised charge, were stranded like islands in a stormy sea, disappearing one by one as they fell to spear thrusts, or to dirkers who jouked under the horses to slash their bellies, the riders being thrown by the rearing mounts, to be stabbed through eye-slits or armour joints. It was merely a matter of

Stirling Bridge 1297

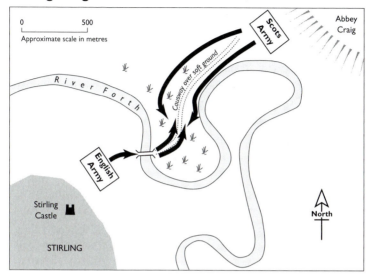

killing till there was no-one left to kill. Many of the Welsh foot, lightly armed, would have been able to plunge into the River Forth, to escape by swimming – their fellows on the southern shore only able to look on in horror as they saw half their army being cut to ribbons. There were some individual acts of valour: Sir Marmaduke Tweng, a knight from Yorkshire, managed to cut his way through the press to the bridge-end and force his horse across its shattered timbers.

Cressingham had been one of the first to cross the bridge. He was obviously of the opinion that the English had only to 'turn up'. He was brought down by a spearman, and with that hatred that Scots have retained for tax-gatherers down the centuries, especially foreign ones, he was stripped and the skin flayed from his body and cut into souvenirs to be taken home and displayed in every town and glen. It is said that one long strip was used to make a sword belt for Wallace himself.

One English chronicler reported that this happened because Cressingham 'was comely and too fat'.

Warenne had had the foresight to remain south of the Forth. He watched more than a hundred men of knightly rank alone perish across the water before turning his horse's head south towards the border. It is said his horse never ate until it reached Berwick, so rapid was his escape. The English on the south bank hurriedly fled with their baggage trains in the direction of Falkirk. James the Steward and Malcolm, Earl of Lennox, suddenly appeared beside these baggage trains with their followers who all this time had been hidden in nearby woodland and decimated the already demoralised survivors.

Politically, this battle achieved nothing, but for the victors the moment must have been exquisite. As I have said above, the English army at this time was the greatest military machine in Christendom. The news of this battle would have spread across Europe like a stone rippling a pond. Never before had an army of gentlemen knights been annihilated by an army of peasant spearmen, whose love for their native heath was enough to outweigh the most expensive military equipment in the world.

On the 700th anniversary of this battle, I stood at Stirling Bridge end and watched direct descendants of Murray and of Scrymgeour, who had remained in Dundee besieging the castle, plant a tree in commemoration of their countrymen. A large crowd sporting Saltires and Lion Rampants appeared, marching behind a piper. They had walked all the way from Dundee, as Wallace's and Murray's men had done, but on this occasion they marched to raise money for a children's charity. As this was taking place, the polling booths across the country were open for voting on Scotland's future. The following day, knowing that there had been a 'yes-yes' vote to the questions asked in the referendum, I was speaking at a *Braveheart* convention in Stirling. It was an emotional affair. The following day I was with Randall Wallace, the scriptwriter of *Braveheart*. The film had been a huge catalyst for the people of Scotland to re-examine their past. I asked him, half-seriously, how it felt to be partly responsible for the impending freedom of a nation. He thought about this for a while, then replied, 'That's a bit heavy to give me responsibility for something as serious as that', then added, 'but at least I can say I did it with the pen – better the pen than the sword!'

The battle site is mostly built over now, although there are some quiet pockets left. The river wends its way through a green area, to the west of the northern end of the old stone bridge. To the east stands Stirling County's rugby ground, with the river flowing past the pitches under the watchful eye of the National Wallace Monument, with its statue of Wallace, sword aloft, surveying the scene of his great victory. But victory at a cost, as Murray received wounds during the battle from which he ultimately did not recover. He was one of the greats of the Wars of Independence who goes sadly unrecognised along with many others. We do not know how much of the victory at Stirling was down to his influence, or how history would have changed if he had lived. He posthumously left a son who was later to be a Guardian of Scotland. It is believed that

Wallace Monument

after his death, which probably happened around the end of 1297, he was taken back to the Black Isle to be buried in Fortrose Cathedral, the ruins of which stand near Chanonry Point in the Moray Firth. (MAP A22)

The National Wallace Monument stands on top of the Abbey Craig, near the spot where Wallace and Murray

Fortrose Cathedral

surveyed the ground before the battle. (MAP B30) The foundations of this monument were laid on 24 June, 1861, when over 80,000 people turned out to see the foundation stone being laid. That is eight to ten times the number of soldiers that Wallace and Murray commanded on the day! The monument was completed in September 1869 and cost £18,000 to build. It was designed by JT Roehead of Glasgow, in the form of a baronial tower, surmounted by a crown. It measures 36ft square at the base and rises to 220ft. The opening took place on 25 June, 1887, when the colossal statue of the national hero was unveiled by the Marquis of Bute. The statue came from the studio of Mr D W Stevenson RSA of Edinburgh.

The monument contains what is believed to be the Wallace's sword. This mighty brand was transferred from Dumbarton Castle in 1888, where it had been left behind after Wallace was captured and taken south.

The sword fit for an archangel to wield,
Was light in his terrible hand.

The sword which is 5ft 7ins long is actually shorter than it was originally. At some point the blade had been broken, and had been repaired by cutting a few inches of steel from the tip, and inserting it inside the broken halves of the blade, enabling them to slide together. The tip was then repointed.

There is a wonderful statue of Wallace in Stirling Town Centre, on the front of the Athenaeum building at the junction of Baker Street and Spittal Street. It depicts Wallace in Grecian style, his mighty sword on his back. It was created by

Handyside Richie in the 1800s, the cost being met by William Drummond. (MAP B29) A bust of Wallace adorns the front of the nearby municipal buildings, and the house known as Viewforth, built for the Drummond family in 1855 and now the headquarters of Stirling Council, has half-lifesize statues of Wallace and Bruce flanking the former main doorway. These statues are carved from

Wallace Statue, Stirling

sandstone and are unfortunately suffering from weather erosion.

77

CHAPTER 9

Invasion

THE SCOTICHRONICON TELLS US that after the victory at Stirling Bridge, Wallace had special lists made up with the names of every able-bodied Scot between sixteen and sixty, so that he could mobilise the entire nation in its defence against England.

A system is said to have been created whereby one man out of five was to be chosen to command the other four and called a quaternion. His commands were to be obeyed in all matters, and whoever did not obey would be killed. There was to be a tenth man, called a decurion, over each nine, and a twentieth over each nineteen, and so on, moving up to one in charge of a thousand, called a chiliarch, and beyond to the top. At the top was the general, whom all were bound to obey to the death. Wallace was chosen as general, and he promised to keep this system until the succession of a legitimate king.

This account of the structure of Wallace's army was written over 140 years later. If there is any truth in it, we can see how the great lords of Scotland would view Wallace as a major threat to the stability of their own feudal system. His overpowering personality had the nobles trembling at their rapid loss of authority. He had broken the iron bonds of feudalism and brought a form of democracy into existence, ignoring the ties of vassalage between the lords and the men who dwelt on their vast estates. Even the hostile English chronicler Hemingburgh remarked:

The whole followers of the nobility had attached themselves to him, and though the persons of their lords were with the King of England, their hearts were with Wallace, who found his army reinforced by so immense a multitude of the Scots that the Community of the land obeyed him as their leader and Prince.

The Cottonian Manuscript reported:

There crowded to Wallace all the Scots of both sexes and all ages, from the boy to the old man, so that in a brief space he had an army which according to their own opinion, no Prince could possibly withstand.

In reading these reports, there is no doubting the truth of the tales of the extraordinary strength of Wallace's conviction. In that age no-one but an invincible fighter could have terrorised and tamed feudal lords as he did.

News reached the Scottish leadership of the fall of the castle at Dundee, the siege left in Scrymgeour's capable hands while the events of Stirling Bridge took place. At this time Wallace is said to have left his army to make a quick sojourn north to Aberdeen, where he hanged, or at least threatened to hang, a few men who had refused to join the cause.

Wallace and his men then embarked on an invasion of northern England, partly in retaliation for wrongs done and partly to strip the wealth from the land to send back to Scotland, where there was real fear of famine that year. En route, Wallace paused at Haddington to write a letter to inform traders abroad that Scotland was again free to trade with foreign ports. (MAP A4) The letter is signed by both Murray and Wallace, although Murray had already been fatally wounded. It was unearthed in the municipal archives of Hamburg many years ago by a Dr Lappenburg. It reads as follows:

> Andrew Murray and William Wallace, Commanders of the Army of Scotland and the Community of the same Kingdom: To the prudent and discreet men and well beloved friends, the Mayors and Commonwealths of Lubeck and Hamburg, greeting and perpetual increase of sincere friendship.
>
> To us it has been intimated by trustworthy Merchants of the said Kingdom of Scotland that as a mark of your regard, you have been favourable to, counselling and assisting in all matters and transactions relating to us and said merchants, though such good offices may not have been preceded by our deserts, and on that account we are more bound to tender you our thanks and a suitable return. This we have willingly engaged ourselves to perform towards you, requesting that, in so far as you cause your Merchants to be informed, they will now have safe access to all the ports of the Kingdom of Scotland with their merchandise, as Scotland, thanks be to God has by war been recovered from the power of the English.
>
> Farewell. Given at Haddington, in Scotland, this 11th day of October 1297.
>
> PS. We have, moreover, to request that you would condescend to forward the interests of our Merchants, John Burnet and John Frere, in their business in like manner as you may wish us to act towards your Merchants in their transactions.
>
> Farewell.

Many such letters were probably sent out to various communities, but at the time of writing, this is the only one we know of. It was displayed at the Glasgow Exhibition of 1911. Although it originally bore two seals, only the one believed to be Murray's survived, with the Royal Arms of Scotland on the front, and a personal device of Murray's on the rear. The letter was subsequently believed lost, perhaps as a consequence of an allied bombing raid on Hamburg during World War II. However, during December 1998 it was re-discovered in a museum in Lübeck. This was an exciting find and makes one wonder if similar documentation is lying, dusty and forgotten, in archives in other museums in Europe.

In a similar vein, an artefact regarded as the epitome of the Wallace cult during Victorian times re-emerged in late 1998. It had at one time been displayed in the National Wallace Monument and consisted of letters from Garibaldi, Kossuth, Mazzini, Blind and Blanc, all speaking of the legacy of Wallace and all written in 1868, and inserted in an exquisitely carved frame fashioned from the famous Wallace Oak of Elderslie. Fortunately, the artefact has been purchased by the Stirling Smith Art Gallery and Museum to save it from being sold at auction, which might have led to it leaving the country.

Blind Harry next has Wallace attacking Cospatrick, the Earl of Dunbar, who consistently fought on the English side during the Wars of Independence. His earldom adjoined England, making it easy for him to be supplied with arms and reinforcements. There is said to have been an engagement at Innerwick, four miles south-east of Dunbar, where Wallace gained the upper hand, and Cospatrick fled to Cockburnpath, before making his escape over the border. (MAP A1)

In late October the Scots invaded Northumberland,

making their base in Rothbury forest. (MAP C7) Vestiges of this forest remain around the village of the same name, which stands south-west of Alnwick. (MAP C8) The cry of 'The Scots are coming' spread terror in the local population, and many fled south into County Durham. The Scots ranged far and wide over both Northumberland and Cumbria. The garrisons of all the major strongholds were able to defy them, the Scots having neither siege-engines nor the resources to construct them. In fact, most of Wallace's men would have had no previous experience of this kind of war, and although they made approaches on Berwick, Alnwick, Newcastle and Carlisle, the garrisons could sit tight and weather the storm, knowing that there was little that the Scots could do. It is said a Scots trumpeter approached the walls of Carlisle, ordering the English inside to surrender and open the city gates or Wallace would destroy them all, but this was merely bravado.

Another window exists at this point to allow us to see the reality of the situation during this incursion onto English soil, for the same story is told in the chronicles of both Guisborough and Heminburgh. Three of the Austin Canons of Hexham had returned to their Abbey even though they knew the Scots were running riot in the surrounding countryside. (MAP C5) Some marauders entered and threatened the monks, demanding to see their treasures. The monks replied that their church had already been visited by others in the Scottish army, and that there was nothing left to take. In the middle of this Wallace arrived, and dismissed the men, telling the monks to prepare to celebrate mass. The monks complied, and Wallace withdrew for a few moments to the vestry to take off some of his armour. Before he reappeared, the men he had sent away sneaked back in and stole the altar ornaments and even the cloth itself.

Wallace was enraged and told his men to find the thieves and hang them, but they only made a pretence of carrying out his orders. Wallace then explained to the monks that many of his men were thorough-going rogues and rascals and beyond his control. This shows the weakness of Wallace's position. Many of his men would respect him as a leader, but they would also see him as equal to themselves and would not follow strict orders as they would with their feudal lords, or show the respect that would be required by their monarch. Wallace then presented the monks with a letter of protection, which ran as follows:

To all the men of the Kingdom of Scotland to whom these present writings shall come – Greeting!
Know ye that, in the name of the King (John Balliol) we have taken the Prior and Convent of Hexham in Northumberland, their lands, their men, and whole possessions, with their effects, movable and immovable, under the firm peace and protection of the said Lord King, and ours.
Wherefore we strictly forbid you to do them any hurt, mischief or injury whatsoever, in their persons, lands, or goods, under penalty of the forfeiture of your own goods and estates to the said Lord the King, or to kill them, or any of them, under pain of losing life and members.
These presents to remain in force for one year to come, and no more.
Given at Hexham, 7th day of November 1297.

We do not know if Wallace wrote this himself or dictated it to a scribe. It is interesting that he mentions that he acts in the name of John Balliol. From what we know of Wallace, he never tried to claim any kind of personal jurisdiction over Scotland. Every act he did was in the name of Scotland's rightful king.

Hexham stands on the A69 between Carlisle and Newcastle, and the abbey is open to visitors. It was founded in 678 AD and its stone crypt is probably the earliest surviving in north-western Europe. The church is dedicated to St Andrew, and I remember the surprise I got, arriving there for the first time, to see a St Andrew's Cross flying from Hexham's topmost tower – I thought the Scots had invaded again!

We know that the Scots also raided Lanercost Priory where the monks kept a chronicle which mentions the Scots arriving, under the command of a 'robber chief' named Wallace, who sacked the premises in November 1297. Lanercost lies some ten miles east of Carlisle, just outside the village of Brampton a mile or so south of Hadrian's Wall. (MAP C4) It stands in a

little vale of the River Irthing, surrounded by extensive ruins, and is still partly used. It is a strange sensation to walk its stone-flagged floors, knowing that

Lanercost Priory

Wallace did so, also Edward Longshanks, who stayed a considerable time here, and Robert the Bruce, who came after Edward's death. The monks at Lanercost seemed to particularly despise Wallace, not so much because he wreaked havoc on the surrounding countryside, but because of his low-born status. The chronicles mention several times that he was not of noble enough stock to warrant any respect. I notice time and again in English sources this lack of respect for men who were fighting for love of their native land. The

English seemed to think that the Scots should have been happy to have Edward and England as their overlord, and that they were doing Scotland a favour.

During the time Wallace remained in England, William Lamberton was elected Bishop of St Andrews on 3 November, 1297. This man was to be a mainstay of the fight for Scottish independence. Along with Robert Wishart, Bishop of Glasgow, he was to become a tower of strength for the Scottish people, assuring them of their right in the face of continued aggression from English prelates. The English accused Wallace of forcing Lamberton's election, but this is obviously quite untrue.

Wallace and his men would appear to have ranged as far west as Cockermouth in their raids on the English countryside, but unfortunately winter came early in 1297, and the Scots were caught by heavy snow and blizzards blocking the roads. A hasty retreat had to be made back across the border. English sources put this unseasonal weather down to divine intervention to teach the ungodly Scots a lesson.

Some time after Wallace's return to Scotland, he was created Guardian. This was unlikely to have had the backing of the bulk of the Scottish nobility, but Wallace had proved himself on the field of battle and in his invasion of England. No-one else came close to him and he was the only choice.

Blind Harry states that he was created Guardian in 'Forest Kirk', and, not unusually, there is some debate as to where this Forest Kirk was located. One or two recent studies have placed it in or near Carluke in Lanarkshire, due to the fact that this parish was named Kirk-Forest in ancient times. It probably got this name from its situation in Maudslie Forest, and the name Carluke may have come into use around Wallace's time, because its church was dedicated to St Luke. There are no traces today of this ancient seat of worship. In my opinion, the name Carluke preceded the time of Wallace – car, or caer, being the old word for a fortification, as in Carlisle or Caernarvon. I am also slightly sceptical because Carluke was not mentioned often during the Wars of Independence, even though it is a place of some antiquity. It would surely have been mentioned more often if it was the site of a building important enough to have contained an assembly capable of electing a Guardian of Scotland. But nothing can be discounted, as there is no proof.

In Selkirk, in the ancient Ettrick Forest, are the remains of the 'Kirk of the Forest' just a few yards from the town centre. (MAP C13) This building carries a large plaque which states it was the site where Wallace was created Guardian. We know that Wallace spent time in the Selkirk area and had a corps of bowmen from there in his army at Falkirk. These factors lend weight to the possibility that the honour of being made Guardian was bestowed upon him in a Selkirk location.

Kirk of the Forest Plaque

It is after this time that he begins to be addressed as Sir William Wallace, and an English chronicler states that he was knighted by one of the 'leading men of Scotland'. His knighthood was probably connected to the occasion of his being created Guardian. Who actually knighted Wallace is a matter for yet more debate. In his excellent novel, *The Wallace*, Nigel Tranter has Robert the Bruce knight Wallace, arriving at this conclusion by a process of elimination. Any knight was capable of creating another, but usually only royalty or leaders of the nobility did so. Nigel Tranter simply worked his way through the earls of Scotland, asking such questions as, who was on the English side? who was too remote? or who was of age (some earldoms being held by minors)? Through this process he arrived at Bruce, but the plain fact is we shall probably never know. Even Blind Harry does not give any clue.

More tellingly, Edward Longshanks had sent a letter to Warenne, the loser at Stirling, which he received around the middle of February 1298, stating that he was returning from Flanders and was personally going to lead the English army against Wallace. Wallace must have known that there would eventually be English retaliation. He may have realised that Edward would lead his army in person, and that arrangements would have to be made to counter this threat.

Torphichen

He had the remainder of the winter and the coming spring to train his men for pitched battle as best he could.

The next we know for certain of Wallace's whereabouts is from a letter to Alexander Scrymgeour, sent from Torphichen in West Lothian in March 1298. (MAP A17) It runs as follows:

We, Sir William Wallace, Guardian of Scotland, by the consent and approbation of the grandees of said kingdom, give and concede, to Alexander, named Scrymgeour, six merks of land in the territory of Dundee, namely, that land which is called the Upper Field, near the town of Dundee. Also the constabulary of the Castle of Dundee, with the rights, liberties, and privileges belonging thereto, without any reservation whatsoever, on performing homage to the forsaid Lord and King, and his heirs and successors, and for the faithful service and assistance rendered to his forsaid kingdom, in bearing the royal standard in the army of Scotland, at the time the present writing has been drawn up. In testimony of which the common seal of the forsaid kingdom of Scotland has been affixed to the present writing.

Given at Torphichen, on the 29th day of March, in the year of grace, 1298.

Scrymgeour was the royal standard bearer in the Scottish army. Unfortunately, he was to suffer the same horrific fate as his master, Wallace, but he left a son, another Alexander, who would carry the Lion Rampant banner behind Robert the Bruce at Bannockburn. There has always been another Scrymgeour to bear this proud honour, and to this day Scrymgeour is Hereditary Standard Bearer of Scotland.

The ancient headquarters of the Knights of St John of Jerusalem stand in Torphichen, and it was probably within these buildings that Wallace's charter to Scrymgeour was written. Today the buildings bear the title, and are signposted, 'Torphichen Preceptory', preceptory meaning 'the base of a subordinate community of the Knights Templars'. The letter quoted above is copied from a facsimile contained within Anderson's *Diplomata et Numismata Scotiae* printed in Edinburgh in 1739.

Blind Harry mentions a couple of events which took place about this time. Wallace's uncle at Dunipace had been captured and was being held prisoner at Airth Castle. (MAP B32) Today, Airth Castle stands on the edge of a whaleback ridge. In Wallace's time this ridge would have been like an island, rising from the marsh surrounding it, part of the River Forth flood plain. Airth village was a port in Wallace's day, but now it stands several hundred yards

Airth Castle

from the shore. A fisherman led Wallace and his men through the marsh; they stormed the castle, slaughtered the garrison, and Wallace freed his uncle whom they found in chains in a vault.

The southern-most part of the later stone castle which occupies the spot today is called the Wallace Tower, and probably stands where the original 'pele' stood. Airth Castle is currently a hotel, the bar being within the Wallace Tower. It is good to enjoy a whisky on the spot where our hero routed a garrison of the invader.

The old church at Airth stands in the trees on the left as you climb the driveway towards the Castle. This church, which was founded in the 1100s, would have been well known to Wallace. It is in a shameful state of neglect, and a little more of it turns to rubble with each passing year. One item of real interest is a tomb dated 1330 surmounted by an effigy of a female in prayer, with what appears to be a little dog at her feet. Its occupant

Mothers Grave

might have remembered Wallace; certainly she would have been alive at the time of Bannockburn. There are many other knightly tombs from the 1500s and 1600s. Close inspection re-veals old date stones, and

Dunfermline Plaque

even a sword and Templar cross inscribed in a wall. At the time of writing, three mort-safes were lying in the graveyard. These were to protect the dead from body-snatchers in the early 1800s.

The other event at about this time was the death of Wallace's mother. She is said to have been buried by John Blair, Wallace's chaplain, and Jop, one of Wallace's most loyal followers, in Dunfermline Abbey churchyard. (MAP A10) A thorn tree now marks the spot, and a plaque in the wall of the Abbots House in Dunfermline commemorates her. Dunfermline Abbey has a magnificent stained glass window showing Bruce (who, along with many other Scottish royals, is buried here), St Margaret, Malcolm Canmore, and Wallace, depicted sword in hand standing guard over Scotia, the spirit of Scotland, depicted as a young woman. This west window is by Sir Noel Paton who in Victorian times submitted plans for a National Wallace Monument which were, however, never used.

In Pittencrieff Glen, between the burn and the ruins of the Royal Palace, lies the Wallace Well. It is quite difficult to find in the under-growth, and is little more than a small stone structure with an iron grill. The reason for its name is lost in the mists of time.

Falkirk

FALKIRK, THE DOUREST, BLOODIEST battle of the Wars of Independence, was to be as responsible for shaping Scotland as the Battle of Bannockburn. For years afterwards its name must have been on many lips. Men would be able to say that they had survived Falkirk which would be met by knowing nods from their fellows. It stands in all its tragedy as a monument to the depth of passion that Scotland can stir in the soul. Scotland was worth fighting for and dying for, that little scrap of moor and mountain on the edge of the world. But Falkirk would also show the ugly side of the coin. Scotland's greatest blight has always been those who do not put her first. They have always been there, throughout her long history. They were there at Falkirk.

Edward was determined to dominate Scotland once and for all. After his humiliation of Balliol and his march to Elgin, his appointment of officers, and the Scots nobility's signatures adorning the Ragman's Roll, he must have gone off to his continental wars in assured mood. When the news of Stirling Bridge came to his ears, it is easy to imagine his angry outburst, particularly when he found out that the leader of the insurrection was a second son of a minor knight and landowner.

Edward made his plans in meticulous fashion. He went as supplicant to the shrine of John of Beverley, and left with his banner to carry before his army. To this banner he added that of St Cuthbert of Durham. This same St Cuthbert had apparently been responsible for the early snow that turned back the Scottish invasion. Propaganda played its part, Wallace being publicised as a thief, a robber, a man who had skinned an Englishman (they got that right at least!). But worst of all, he was falsely depicted as being the type of man who would abandon his comrades with a heartless jest. That the Scots were willing to stand up for their country's freedom seems to have shocked the English chroniclers. To them Wallace was the scum of the earth. They could not seem to grasp the fact that Wallace's men were there for love of him and Scotland. To them the Scots were shameful brigands who defied good King Edward's magnanimity.

Edward marched north, following the north-east coast of England through Newcastle and Alnwick and crossed the border into Scotland in early July 1298, pausing at Roxburgh. He had roughly 2,000 heavy cavalry and 12,000 foot soldiers. They advanced through Lauderdale and over Soutra to the outskirts of Edinburgh, which they reached on 11 July. Wallace retired before them. It seems he was deliberately pulling the English army on. The land had been devastated. It was said that in all Lothian the English had been able to find only one skinny cow. 'The dearest beef I have ever seen', remarked the Earl of Surrey dryly. If Wallace wanted to wear the enemy down through marching, starvation and lack of an enemy to fight, it would seem he came close to achieving his aim. Because of the result of the Battle of Falkirk, we overlook the plan that Wallace had put into action, which came so very close to victory without battle even being joined.

There is a little tale which is worth repeating here; behind Cumbernauld, on the road to Airdrie, there stands a tiny village named Riggend. (MAP B26) Travelling south to Airdrie and

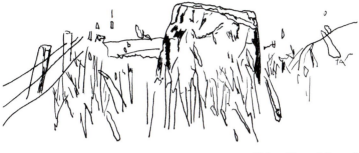

Wallace Stone at Riggend

taking the small road to the right as you enter the village, a mile or so down this road a large boulder can be seen, standing on the left in the corner of a field. Although very tenuous, the story that has been handed down the generations is that this boulder is where Wallace sharpened his sword before the Battle of Falkirk. The road here follows the line of an old drove road which continued over the moorland toward Slamannan, then on by Glen Ellrig House to Shieldhall and Falkirk. It is possible that Wallace led his troops this way before the battle, and once camped, knowing that a confrontation was due, his men would keep their weapons honed, and where better to do this than on a kenspeckle big stone?

This is all very much supposition, but it is important that sites like this are not lost to us. An old historical sketch of Airdrie states that this was where 'Wallace sharpened his twa-edged claythorn'.

Edward sent Bishop Anthony Beck to capture the castles of East Lothian that were held by the Scots. Beck had no siege engines and sent Sir John Fitz-Marmaduke back to King Edward to ask what he should do. Edward, tellingly, replied, 'You are a bloodthirsty man. I have often had to rebuke you for being too cruel. But now be off and use all your cruelty, and instead of rebuking you, I shall praise you.' Dirleton Castle which still stands in the village of the same name fell within two days, and the others two days later. But Edward's army was starving. They must have been despairing of the arrival of the transport ships which he had organised to follow and supply his men. Some ships arrived at Leith, but they contained only wine. Making a rare mistake, Edward had this rationed out to the troops. Drunk, his Welsh footmen killed some English priests and had to be charged by heavy cavalry: 80 Welshmen were killed. When informed that the Welsh were threatening to go over to the Scots, Edward is reported to have said, 'What does it matter, let them join the Scots, then I will defeat them all in one go.'

On 21 July, when the English were camped at Temple Liston and Kirkliston, two Scottish Earls, Dunbar and Angus, rode into the English camp. (MAP A7) When they heard that the English were getting ready to retreat to Edinburgh, they informed them that the Scottish army was no more than 18 miles away at Falkirk. It has been supposed that Wallace was waiting for the English to retreat before falling on them. He might have succeeded in his ploy, but we will never know. Two traitors were to be responsible for thousands of Scottish deaths.

Edward readied his men, and marched along the road towards Falkirk. They camped that night on the Burgh Muir of Linlithgow. (MAP A8) Burghmuir Farm still exists to the east of the town, and it would have been in the fields around this farm that the English army bivouaked.

Behind Linlithgow is a prominent hill named Cockleroy. (It is only a short haul to the summit from the nature trail in Beecraigs Country Park.) (MAP A16) The dip between its summits is called Wallace's Cradle. Tradition has it that Wallace watched the enemy camp from here. The view is astonishing. It stretches from the Bass Rock in the east to Ben Lui in the far north-west. All Linlithgow is laid out like a map below. It is easy to imagine Wallace, assessing enemy numbers and calculating. Not only did he have a country to guard and a terrible enemy to defeat, but he was plagued with turncoats.

During the night, Edward was trampled by his horse. There was alarm in the camp that perhaps the Scots had attacked in the night. Edward immediately got ready and mounted his horse, even though he was in pain, to show his men he was unharmed, and early in the morning of Tuesday, 22 July, he marched his army on.

There are no prominent landmarks at Falkirk as there are at Stirling, with its bridge and the Abbey Craig, so there will always be speculation regarding the site of the battle. I shall put forward some personal theories, taking into account local tradition.

As the English advanced towards Falkirk in the early morning mist and gloom, perhaps making their way through the area where the village of Maddiston now stands, it is

Wallace Stone

reported that Scots spearmen were spotted on a hill. Some writers have speculated that this was a party of Scots making their way to join Wallace. However, high on a ridge south-east of Falkirk stands the village of Wallacestone, and tradition has it that Wallace stood here on a large boulder to spy out the surrounding territory. (MAP B33) Over the years this Wallacestone has disappeared like so many other Wallace artefacts, perhaps chipped away piece by piece for souvenirs. In 1810, a 10ft high pillar was erected to mark the spot, just a little east of the site of the stone. The view from this pillar is immense, taking in the Forth and all the low lying ground in the Falkirk area.

If Wallace stood here with a body of troops to watch for the English advance as legend states, this may have been the group of spearmen that the English saw. It is recorded that a party of English knights galloped to the spot, only to find the Scots had disappeared. Professor Barrow suggests that the Scots army stood with the Westquarter Burn in front and Callendar Wood to their rear – this vicinity is today the site of Woodend Farm. From Wallacestone one can just discern Woodend Farm a mile or two to the north-west, and it is my belief that Wallace stood at Wallacestone to watch for the English approach, but at the same time was able to turn 180° to see his schiltroms (circles of spearmen) in the distance on the hillside above the junction of the Westquarter and Hallglen burns. Perhaps he could not see them too clearly, as it was early morning and may have been misty in the gut of the Westquarter.

Edward's troops pushed on a little and had started to pitch tents for mass to be celebrated, when in the growing light, they suddenly saw the Scots preparing for battle.

The chronicle of Guisborough states that the Scots were sited on hard ground on one side of a hill beside Falkirk, facing south-east. The Scalacronica states that they were on 'this side of Falkirk' meaning the side of Falkirk facing in the direction of Linlithgow. The gradient of the hillside where Woodend Farm stands has changed over the years, partly due to farm building, but mostly due to a modern road being built across the slope. It is also recorded that the Scots' front was protected by a 'boggy loch'. In the valley floor below Woodend Farm, where the Westquarter Burn runs and meets the burn from Hallglen, we can see that the ground would once have been very marshy before modern farm drainage. Housing is now encroaching across this area.

The chronicle of Guisborough gives a very exact description of how the Scots disposed themselves for the forthcoming battle. The Scots had formed themselves into four great schiltroms, hedgehog fashion. Each schiltrom contained about 2,000 men. Round each were wooden stakes interlaced with ropes to break up charging cavalry. In between the schiltroms stood the archers from the forest of Selkirk under Sir John Stewart. What cavalry Wallace had was under the command of various lords, most notably Sir John Comyn.

The English heavy cavalry surged forward to attack the schiltroms, unaware of the existence of the boggy loch. They hit the edge of it and the horses sank in under the weight of their armour-clad riders. To find a way round, they turned right and left, east and west. The party to the east was under the leadership of Bishop Anthony Beck, with 36 senior commanders of cavalry. The party to the west was under the Earls of Norfolk, Lincoln and Hereford. As they made their way around the watery obstacle and began to charge the Scots, Wallace shouted to his men, 'I have brought you to the ring, dance the best you can!'

As the English lowered their lances to make contact with the Scots spearmen, the Scots cavalry turned and fled the field. This act has been the subject of much debate. Was it because they were men of the upper classes, jealous of the lowly Wallace's elevated station? Was it caused by panic and fright atthe sight of the cream of England's chivalry in full attack? Much has been made of the fact that Comyn was present. Did he play a part in the decision to flee the field? Whatever the reason, the cavalry left the schiltroms alone and exposed. The first to suffer were the archers. Sir John

Stewart was ridden down with his men; they had no defence against a heavy cavalry charge.

The English tried to break into the schiltroms, but the Scots stood firm. The peasants with their spears showed the bravery that their mounted 'superiors' had so crucially lacked. A list survives of the 120 English horses lost and testifies to the fact that the cavalry could not break the spearmen. But Edward had a weapon against which the Scots had no defence. From the far side of the boggy loch, English archers could fire into the mass of spearmen. It was said that each English longbowman carried a dozen Scots' lives under his belt. Each archer could have several arrows in flight at once, steel-tipped projectiles capable of piercing armour at 600 yards. We can picture Edward looking with satisfaction across the valley of the Westquarter as he watched the schiltroms deteriorate.

Falkirk 1298

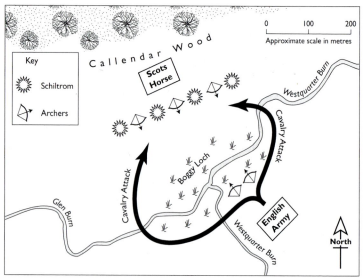

Wallace, reddened sword in hand, his apprehension growing, would have been yelling encouragement to his spearmen. Their bravery was astonishing, bringing down charge after charge of horse; they were immovable. But when the arrows began to rain down, it was a different matter. Gaps opened in the ranks and steel-clad English horsemen, armed with mace or axe, plunged in. Somewhere in all this carnage, Sir John the Graham fell. It is said Wallace shed tears over the body of his comrade.

Inevitably, with the schiltroms disintegrating, men tried to reach the cover of Callendar Wood. Wallace was one of the lucky ones. He reached the woodland, but he must have been kenspeckle on the battlefield, Scrymgeour at his back, the Lion Rampant banner flapping on the breeze. Sir Brian le Jay, the Master of the English Templars, followed him into the wood, where Wallace is said to have killed him.

Edward was master of the field, a field littered with thousands of dead. He had won the day, but his satisfaction must have been tinged with sorrow and anger at Wallace's escape.

Bruce learned lessons from Falkirk. At Bannockburn he kept the cavalry in reserve, and as English archers massed to release their deadly hail, his cavalry smashed them to pieces. Wallace may have had the same idea, but his horsemen had abandoned him. For years historians have argued about Bruce's part during the Battle of Falkirk. Blind Harry has Bruce fighting with the English; after the battle he met Wallace at Dunipace. Wallace berated him for not seeing the truth sooner, and Bruce realised he had betrayed the country of his birth.

However, we know that when Edward reached Ayr in August, the castle had been burnt by Bruce so that it would afford no shelter to the English. This is not really what one would expect from a man who had fought with Edward the previous month. So the possibility remains that Bruce fought with Wallace at Falkirk.

Only two Englishmen of any note were slain at Falkirk, the Master of the English Templars, and the Master of the Scottish Templars, who fought with Edward. He had been born in Huntingdonshire. The Scots would have to learn not to allow Englishmen such positions of authority in Scotland, where they could attack from within.

There are several sites in Falkirk that have a connection with the battle apart from the pillar at Wallacestone. This pillar is the focus for a ten-mile march each year by the Sir William Wallace Grand Lodge of Free Colliers of Falkirk who raise money from their effort for charity.

The churchyard at Falkirk which occupies an ancient site contains three monuments to the slain. (MAP B33) Sir John the Graham, Wallace's good friend, lies here. His tomb stands yards from the bustling pedestrian precinct of the town centre. It is surrounded by an iron railing made by the men of the Carron Iron Works. Above it is a casting of Sir John's two-handed sword which still survives. The tomb is in a decaying state, and the cast of the sword is broken. The gravestone has been thrice renewed, the new stones being laid on top of the old. They all bear the same inscription:

Here lies Sir John the Grame, baith wight and wise
Ane of the chiefs who reschewit Scotland thrice
Ane better knight not to the world was lent
Nor was gude Grame of truth and hardiment

The area of Grahamston in Falkirk is named after Sir John the Graham. A monument to him stands in Victoria Park, north of the road heading towards Grangemouth. The edifice, a square granite block surmounted by the Lion Rampant, was raised in 1912, paid for by Robert Dollar, resident of San Francisco but native of Falkirk. The inscription says that Graham fell near this spot, but this would seem unlikely.

Lying flat at a corner of the church, near the tomb of Sir John the Graham, is the tomb of Sir John Stewart, who fell with his archers between the schiltroms, brought down by an English lance. In 1877, his descendant, the Marquis of Bute, erected a monument in the graveyard, a granite Celtic cross, with the inscription:

> In memory of the men of Bute who under Sir John Stuart on the 22 July 1298 near the Fawekirk fought bravely and fell gloriously.

Monument at Falkirk Churchyard to the men of Bute

Before we leave Falkirk, there is an alternative battle-site to be considered. In his 1948 book, *William Wallace, Guardian of Scotland*, James Fergusson put forward a theory that the battle was fought over the infant River Avon, rather than the Westquarter. This site stands a further three or four miles south. I am doubtful that a battle fought so far distant would be called the Battle of Falkirk, but there are one or two things worth recording regarding this site.

Mentioned earlier is the stone at Riggend where Wallace is said to have sharpened his sword. The old drove road from Riggend to Falkirk ran by Glen Elrig House, which was demolished around 1990 and is now a landfill site. (MAP B34)

Fergusson reckoned the Scottish schiltroms were positioned where this house once stood. A standing stone survives, and local tradition says that it marks the burial site of the English horses killed at Falkirk. No-one would have used fit horses to drag dead horses all this distance to bury them. They would have been buried on or near the battlefield itself. I contacted the landfill site manager who informed me that no remains were discovered when the top layers of soil were removed for operational work. He was conscientious regarding ancient remains, and had avoided the standing stone. He told me that there had originally been two standing stones, and it is possible that these marked a battle of some sort.

Two lesser known stones which stand in the grounds of the police station at Randolphsfield in Stirling are said to mark where Randolph's schiltrom held the English charge at Bannockburn. Perhaps Randolph merely told his men to halt at the stones, but if there was a tradition of marking battle sites with stones during this era, the ones at Glen Elrig are intriguing, the more so as the nearby farmhouse bears the name Redbrae. This could refer to the appearance of the hillside after a battle. The story that the English horses were buried at Glen Elrig may only date from the time of Fergusson's book, the idea that this was a battle site embedding itself in the local psyche.

The Ordnance Gazetteer of Scotland from the 1890s puts the battle-site 'midway between the River Carron and the town', roughly where the Forth and Clyde canal stands today. I find this improbable as there are no features there that fit with the few facts we have.

This leaves the Westquarter-Woodend Farm site as the most probable to me and to others. I have introduced Wallacestone into the equation as the possible site where the group of Scots spearmen were spotted.

Lanercost Priory
Wallace was here during his invasion of England. Longshanks spent his last months in the 'Guesthouse'.

Glasgow Cathedral
Bishop Wishart's tomb is contained here, to the rear of the building.

Dumbarton Castle

It is believed Wallace was held captive here before his journey south in chains to his execution at Smithfield in London.

Roslyn Castle
The Battle of Roslyn was fought in the vicinity.

One of the many supposed likenesses of Wallace.

Carlisle Castle

Wallace made a half-hearted attempt to besiege Carlisle during his invasion of England.

The Laying of the Foundation Stone of the National Wallace Monument
80,000 people climbed to the summit of the Abbey Craig to see the first stone laid of the Monument to 'Scotland's Hero'!

The Wallace Monument, Robroyston

Site of Wallace's capture in August 1305. This is the opening ceremony in 1900. Note the sword-shaped garland of flowers bearing the legend 'Freedom'.

The Wallace Well, Robroyston

This photograph of the well situated near the barn where Wallace was captured was probably taken around the turn of the 20th Century. The site has since been landscaped.

Newcastle
Part of Wallace's body was displayed here.

Wallace Statue, Baltimore, U.S.A.
This statue of Wallace in Druid Hill Park was unveiled in 1893.

Wallace Monument
A rare photograph of the construction of the National Wallace Monument
atop the Abbey Craig. Note the railway constructed to carry the stone
from the nearby quarry.

CHAPTER 11

Missions Abroad

WE KNOW VERY LITTLE of Wallace's life during the seven years he lived after the Battle of Falkirk. Certainly he was no longer Guardian. It is possible that this honour was taken away from him, but it is more likely he resigned. The carnage of the Battle of Falkirk would have affected him deeply, and he would probably rather have been seen as a common soldier from then on, fighting with his fellows for better or worse, than having command over their destiny.

After the battle, Edward stayed at Torphichen, where Wallace had written the letter to Scrymgeour before the battle. (MAP A17) Edward may have been there to receive treatment for his ribs, damaged when he was trampled by his horse, from the Knights of St John, as they were regarded as the best medical men in those days.

During this time, Wallace is alleged to have hidden with a few followers in a cave on the River Avon, so that he could keep an eye on Edward's movements. (This has a parallel with *Braveheart*, where we see Wallace and a few companions injured and resting by a river after the battle.) The cave, called Wallace's Cave, is roughly a mile upstream from the point where the bridge carries the Falkirk to Bathgate road across the Avon Gorge. (MAP B35) It is signposted from the B8047, east of Westfield village, just before the roundabout where it meets the A801. Much of the roof has collapsed but it must have been quite roomy and there was access at either end, in case a quick escape was required. Adjacent is a wooden footbridge over the

Avon which has gained the name The Wallace Bridge from its proximity to the cave.

The post of Guardian was filled by Robert the Bruce and John Comyn (who had fled the field of Falkirk) as co-holders. Bruce and Comyn always seem to have behaved like two dogs eyeing the one bone. Bruce was eventually to stab Comyn to death in Dumfries before assuming the crown of Scotland. Written evidence has survived which shows the relationship between these two, and more importantly, has Wallace as the subject. The English constable of Roxburgh Castle, Robert Hastang, had a spy in the Scots army. Hastang wrote to Edward regarding an incident which had taken place at a council in Peebles in August 1299:

> At the council Sir David Graham demanded the lands and goods of Sir William Wallace because he was leaving the kingdom without the leave or approval of the Guardians. And Sir Malcolm, Wallace's brother, answered that neither his lands or his goods should be given away, for they were protected by the peace in which Wallace had left the kingdom, since he was leaving to work for the good of the kingdom. At this, the two knights gave the lie to each other and drew their daggers. And since Sir David Graham was of Sir John Comyn's following and Sir Malcolm Wallace of the Earl of Carrick's following, it was reported to the Earl of Buchan and John Comyn that a fight had broken out without their knowing it, and John Comyn leaped at the Earl of Carrick and seized him by the throat, and the Earl of Buchan turned on the bisop of St Andrews, declaring that treason and lese-majestie were being plotted. Eventually the Stewart and others came between them and quietened them...

This letter is the first real piece of information we have about Wallace after Falkirk. We can only guess at his movements during the year that had elapsed. We do know he travelled abroad, to put Scotland's case to the courts of foreign monarchs, and this letter lets us see that he was planning a trip in the late summer of 1299. What is also intriguing from the letter is the relationship between Wallace's brother, Malcolm, and Bruce, who was Earl of Carrick. Malcolm seems to have attached himself to Bruce's following, as several incidents known to us testify. This is not bizarre, as they were both south-western Scots families, and it does give us a small insight into Wallace's relationship with Robert the Bruce.

Blind Harry describes Wallace setting sail from Dundee accompanied by Blair, his chaplain, Jop and Kerlie, amongst others. On his trip across the North Sea, Harry tells us of Wallace's encounter with John of Lynn, a notorious English pirate, who Wallace defeated in a fight at sea. Harry has Wallace making two trips abroad, defeating the pirate Thomas de Longueville on the first. These two stories are so similar, that with the time-scale involved, Harry is probably recounting two versions of the same tale.

When Wallace was finally captured, he had various letters on his person, including documents of safe conduct issued by King Haakon of Norway and King Philip of France. These documents are lost. We do not know if he visited Norway, or if he went to Orkney or Shetland, at that time under Norway's jurisdiction.

We do know that Wallace visited France to elicit French aid for Scotland's cause, and perhaps to visit the deposed King, Balliol, who was at this time living in France. While there, Harry has Wallace fight and defeat a lion, among other adventures. The only proof of his stay in France are a few records of payments on his behalf from the French exchequer. It would be interesting to know how he was perceived at the French court. Wallace remained in France until the tail-end of the year 1300.

We can imagine what a wrench it must have been for him to have left his beloved Scotland. His passion for Scottish nationhood would have driven him on to do his best on Scotland's behalf. He would have worried about the state of the country and fretted over the machinations of some of his own countrymen.

On 7 November, 1300, Philip IV of France granted Wallace a letter of recommendation to be presented to French officials at Rome. It was worded as follows:

> Philip by Grace of God, King of the French, to my beloved and trusting agents appointed to the court of Rome, greetings and love. We command you to request the Supreme Pontiff to hold our beloved William Wallace of Scotland, Knight, recommended to his favour in those matters of business that he has to despatch with him.

Wallace the diplomat is an intriguing picture. This soldier, accustomed to peril, used to sleeping rough during his many campaigns, must surely have found it strange that he, second son of a small Renfrewshire knight, was visiting the home of the most potent power of the western world. The Church was the one authority that even Edward of England feared, and if Scotland could be served thereby, we can be sure that Wallace would see this as another campaign to be fought with as much confidence as possible. From Rome, it is understood that Wallace made his way back to the King of France, en route for his homeland.

Edward of England had not been idle while Wallace was absent. He invaded south-western Scotland and laid seige to Caerlaverock Castle south of Dumfries, and although the garrison asked for honourable surrender terms, Edward stormed the castle and hung them from the nearest trees. (MAP B1) His army then skirmished with the Scots on the Cree estuary, between Creetown and Newton Stewart. (MAP B4) A letter came to Edward from the Pope, rebuking him for his behaviour towards Scotland. The letter was probably the result of Wallace's work abroad, and led to a parley taking place between Edward and the Scots at which Edward treated the Scots with disdain. He said, 'Every one of you has done homage to me as chief lord of Scotland, now you make a fool of me as if I were a weakling.' The Scots replied, 'You should not laugh. Exert your strength and see if might will triumph over right or right over might.' Edward's reply to this was that he would waste Scotland from sea to sea and make its people submit to him.

There is a tale that Wallace was imprisoned by Philip of France before his return to Scotland. Philip seemed to feel that Wallace would be a useful pawn in his negotiations with Edward, and it appears he considered handing Wallace over to the English authorities. For whatever reason, this obviously never transpired, and Wallace managed to find a ship to take him back to Scotland, landing according to Harry on the banks of the Firth of Tay.

From acting as an envoy in warm foreign climes, Wallace had returned home to live as a guerilla fighter. He was always prepared to commit himself to the hard life that Scotland's freedom required from him. He had been absent for perhaps three years. It was now the year of our Lord, 1303.

CHAPTER 12

Final Years

AN ENGLISH FORCE, commanded by Sir John Segrave and accompanied by Ralph Manton, had just reached Roslin, south of Edinburgh, on 24 February, 1303, when it was caught by a surprise attack. (MAP A6) The Scots, led by Comyn and Sir Simon Fraser, had ridden all night from Biggar (it is perhaps this battle that Harry misplaces as having taken place at Biggar). There is a possibility that Wallace was present. The all-night ride certainly has his stamp on it. The English chronicler Rishanger mistakenly describes Wallace as being the leader of the Scots.

The first mention of Wallace after his return for which there is proof is the report that he issued from the Forest of Selkirk to raid into Annandale, Liddesdale and even over the border into Cumberland. He was accompanied in this by Sir Simon Fraser and John Comyn, so he may have been present at Roslin.

Edward's hold on Scotland was growing tighter. He advanced his forces through the country, many Scots making submission to him. He wintered from November 1303 to February 1304 at Dunfermline. Edward showed leniency to those who had recently taken arms against him. This encouraged many, and soon very few remained committed to the Scottish cause, in deed at least. While at Dunfermline Edward sent a mounted force into the Forest of Selkirk to try and capture Wallace. This was led by Segrave, who had escaped at Roslin, together with Clifford and Latimer, and they surprised Wallace and Sir Simon Fraser and a small force of men at Happrew near Peebles. Apparently, things were touch and go, but Wallace and Fraser managed to cut their way through the English and make their escape into the surrounding hills. Many of their men were killed.

The name Happrew survives today in the farms of Easter and Wester Happrew, some four miles west of Peebles. (MAP C15) Above the Lyne Water, just after the A72 crosses it going eastwards, to the north of the road are the remains of a well-preserved Roman fort. I have often wondered whether Wallace and Fraser were using it as a camp when they were surprised. Certainly it makes a good place to view the nearby terrain.

Things were becoming more desperate for Wallace with every passing week. Scots seeking reconciliation with Edward were told that he would look upon them more kindly if they betrayed Wallace. Edward stated that 'the Stewart, Sir John de Soules and Sir Ingram de Umfraville are not to have safe-conducts or come within his power until Sir William Wallace is given up'.

Wallace's last recorded fight before his capture was in September 1304 at Black Earnside or Ironside. (MAP A11) The English were led by Sir Aymer de Valence, an experienced soldier. Although heavily outnumbered, Wallace and his small band managed to inflict casualties on the enemy before escaping. The site of this skirmish is reported to be in the area between Abernethy and Lindores, under the north-eastern outliers of the Ochil Hills. The name Black Earnside comes from the fact that this area was formerly covered by thick forest which stretched some eight or nine miles eastwards from the confluence of the rivers Earn and Tay. The name was probably coined from the deep gloom of the trees. The forest was destroyed long ago, but until recently farm machinery was still uncovering large pieces of black oak.

The local residents in Newburgh believe that the fight took place on the hillside immediately south-east of the ruins of Lindores Abbey. As if to lend some credence to this legend, the remains of a couple of swords were discovered there some years ago. Local people also informed me that Wallace hid in a small tunnel after the battle, and that this tunnel still existed. If you follow the farm road by Lindores Abbey in the direction of Balmerino, a mile along the road is an S-bend, and beneath the roadway there is a small stone tunnel. It looks to be of a later date than Wallace's time, but I am interested as much in the legends as in the history of Wallace.

Time was running out for him. It seems that even Sir Simon Fraser eventually submitted to Edward. A document exists which states, 'Sir Simon Fraser, Sir John Comyn, Sir Alexander Lindsay and Sir David Graham are to exert themselves until twenty days after Christmas (1304) to capture William Wallace and hand him over to the king. And the king will take careful note of how each conducts himself, so that he may show most favour to the one who takes him, with regard to mitigation of his sentence to exile or fine.' From that Christmas till his capture in August 1305, we can only imagine how perilous life must have been for him. If he still retained a small band of patriots about him, they must have been very desperate and dangerous men. They would not know who to trust, and would probably be ready to act first and ask questions afterwards in most situations. Wallace, if he could have managed to hire a ship, could probably have ended his days abroad as a soldier in some continental war. But we know enough of him to know that he believed in himself, and in Scotland, and that he would not be turned aside from his life's work. He may have imagined that his life would end quickly in battle. He was, in fact, to be part of a show trial held in London. As he sat, hungry and cold and trying to find shelter from relentless rain, he could never have imagined that 700 years later people in Scotland would revere his memory. Wallace was following his heart, and he stayed true to that heart to the end.

CHAPTER 13

The Last Days

THE END CAME FOR Wallace in August 1305. He may well have been in the Glasgow area to make contact with Robert Wishart, the patriotic Bishop of Glasgow. Wallace had been helped by Wishart in the past, and with the situation becoming ever more desperate, he may have hoped that the Bishop might help with money or sustenance.

I remember as a child walking round Glasgow Cathedral with a guide. When we reached the steps at the rear of the building I recall him telling me, 'Wallace used to sit on these stairs, waiting for Wishart, who was the Bishop here'. It is funny how little details like this stick in your mind.

Glasgow Cathedral is an ancient edifice, the present stone structure having been consecrated in 1197. Wishart was buried here, and his effigy stands at the rear of the lower church, at the side of the chapel of St Andrew. (MAP B22) His tomb has no sign and lies defaced, in contrast to the memorials lining the church, erected by those rich enough to purchase them, and the many battle honours of the British army. Wishart Street at the rear of the cathedral is named after him. I feel that the man who aided Wallace, absolved Bruce from the murder of Comyn, and presided at Bruce's coronation should be better remembered.

Wallace spent the night before his capture at a farm outside the city, on land belonging to Glasgow Cathedral. The nearby area of Bishopbriggs takes its name from this church land, ie, the bishop's 'riggs' or fields. Wallace slept in the barn, accompanied by Kerlie, his faithful companion. Apparently, the barn was surrounded by soldiers around midnight on 3 August (many historians mention the 3rd, although the date on the monument is the 5th). Wallace had finally been betrayed. Kerlie was stabbed to death on the spot. Wallace was chained, and seeing what had happened to Kerlie, he would have been under no illusions that his end had come. His betrayer was a Scot, Sir John Menteith. He had come into Edward Longshank's peace in 1304, and Edward had granted him the wardenship of Dumbarton Castle, and made him sheriff there. As already stated, Edward had made Wallace's capture one of his stipulations when making his peace with various Scots lords. Most of them probably made some half-hearted gesture in this direction, but Menteith ensured that he went down in history as the 'False Menteith', betrayer of William Wallace.

Tradition has it that Menteith had two accomplices who reported on Wallace's movements. They were named as Jack Short, who had apparently joined Wallace's band under false pretences, and Ralph Ray or Raa, after whom Robroyston (Ralph-Raa's-town) was named. The actual spot of Wallace's capture was in Robroyston itself, near where the later Robroyston Hospital was built. (MAP B23)

The barn was demolished many years ago, but someone was astute enough to keep some of the wood from its rafters, and this was made into a chair which has survived (and can now been seen in Sir Walter Scott's house at Abbotsford).

A derelict farm which probably lies on the site of the one from Wallace's time stands opposite the beautiful monument raised to mark the spot of Wallace's capture. It is in the style of a Celtic cross with a mighty sword embossed on the front. A plaque on the cairn beneath gives the details of his capture.

Much of the money raised for this monument came from a public subscription fund begun by the Reverend David MacRae of the Scottish Patriotic Society. The monument was unveiled at a ceremony in 1900, attended by a large crowd. Old photographs of the ceremony show a garland of flowers hanging from one of the trees nearby, stating the word 'Freedom'. The spectators would have been surprised to know that 95 years later, after the film *Braveheart* was released, the simple word 'Freedom' would become a catch-

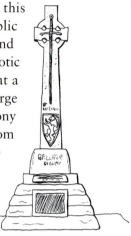

Monument at Robroyston

phrase shouted passionately on many occasions when Scotland's future is the topic. When I ask people for directions to sites connected with Wallace, they happily oblige and, nine times out of ten, then say 'Freedom'.

The Clan Wallace Society of North America paid for the restoration of the monument in September 1986. The plaque testifying to this was stolen in 1996. As it was attached to a large granite block, it could not have been easy lifting it over the surrounding railings! The monument stood until recently amid rolling farmland, but housing estates are slowly encroaching on the site. Because of this, the access by road is constantly changing. The best way to find it is to travel east on the M8 from Glasgow city centre and take the M80 turn-off, then take the Bishopbriggs slip road from the M80. The monument stands about a mile north from this point.

A few hundred yards from the monument is the Wallace Well. This little spring is now landscaped, with a few steps leading from the road to its walled site. What its connection is with Wallace, I have never been able to fathom. Perhaps Wallace had his last drink as a free man here. I remember visiting the monument and the well late one night in 1997, the comet Hale-Bopp spreading its tail across the clear sky. This was probably the last time that the stars would be so visible from this spot, as the street lights of the city are creeping ever nearer.

The Society of William Wallace campaigned to get the developers at least to give a nod to the sanctity of the historic site and they agreed to give some of the streets Wallace-related names. The Wallace legend continues to grow, with one of the nearer developments being named 'Murron's Lea' after Wallace's sweetheart in *Braveheart*.

After his capture at Robroyston, Wallace was taken to Dumbarton Castle. (MAP B20) Part of the castle is still known as Wallace's Prison, and it may be that he was held captive in this building. It was certainly being referred to as 'Wallace's Tower' in the early 1500s, but all the older buildings are now in ruins.

Dumbarton Rock

The castle is open to the public. When climbing the steep steps towards the top, a contorted carved face can be seen just under the roof of one of the guard houses. Local children point this out as the face of the 'False Menteith'. It has always been said that the Lake of Menteith, the only lake in Scotland, is so called because a loch could not be named after such a traitor. Many historians have tried to exonerate Menteith, saying he was only doing his duty as Edward's man. But he was a Scot who delivered another Scot into foreign hands to suffer a hideous death, and for that there can be no excuse. Wallace himself despised all traitors, and I am of like disposition.

When Wallace was taken south, his sword was left behind at Dumbarton and remained there until its transfer to the Wallace Monument on the Abbey Craig in 1888. The authenticity of this weapon is yet another subject of debate that can never be satisfactorily cleared up. There are records from the time of James IV of money being set aside for the 'upkeep of Wallace's sword'. Records from Dumbarton include an inventory compiled by one Sempill, dated 31 May, 1644, that states that there was in Wallace Tower 'an auld two handed sward without a scabbard'. When Dorothy Wordsworth and Samuel Coleridge visited Dumbarton Castle during their travels in 1803, they stated that they were shown a large rusty weapon called Wallace's Sword. When the sword was eventually handed over to Dr Rogers, who had the duty of transferring it to the Wallace Monument, the Colonel who handed it over stated emotionally that by delivering this sword to Dr Rogers, 'he had conferred on him the highest honour it was possible for the British government to bestow on any native of our northern kingdom'.

Up to the time when the sword was moved, bands on board Clyde steamers would strike up *Scots wha hae* as they passed the Dumbarton Castle rock, but this ceased when the sword was taken to Stirling.

When Wallace left Dumbarton Castle, he was smuggled to the border by the most remote roads. Obviously his captors must have assumed that his friends might try to liberate him, but it is doubtful if any of them even knew he had been captured.

A bizarre story exists regarding the start of his journey south to London. I had been told that, after crossing the Clyde from Dumbarton, Wallace had been chained to a tree somewhere behind Port Glasgow, and that this tree still stood with the chain around it. (MAP B19) To try to find the truth behind this, I drove to the southern side of Port Glasgow and questioned various passers-by. Yes, they had heard of the tree, but everyone I spoke to placed it in a different location, and each site I checked had no trees of such antiquity. I then asked another man walking his dog, and he replied that if I just walked a few yards with him, he would show me the spot. He led me into the grounds of the Holy Family Presbytery in Parkhill Avenue and pointed to a patch of disturbed ground. He informed me that an ancient oak had stood on this spot until it had fallen some eighteen months before in 1995. He told me that the churchmen in the presbytery had done everything in their power to save the tree, fencing it off and erecting supports, but to no avail. And yes, there had been a chain around the tree! He informed me that when the chain rusted away, it was always replaced with another, the last one being in Victorian days. He added that the priest who had tried his utmost to save the tree was based in Howwood in Renfrewshire, and as far as he knew, had taken the chain with him. It may be a legend, but a story like this must be saved for posterity, and I took some slides of the tree site while there were still traces of its location.

Wallace was taken to the Solway Firth, where he was

handed over to Sir Aymer de Valence and Sir Robert Clifford who took him to Carlisle. He was then handed over to Sir John Segrave, who had attacked Wallace at Happrew, for the journey on to London. As the party did not arrive in London until Sunday, 22 August, we can picture Wallace, chained to his horse, being led through various towns and villages on the road south, an object of ridicule.

Once in London, Wallace was taken to the presence of Edward Longshanks, who refused to see him. Historians have pondered whether these two ever came face to face. He was then lodged for the night in the house of an alderman of London named William de Leyre, somewhere in the parish of St Gabriel's in Fenchurch Street. It is said that the crowds were so great that he could not be taken to the Tower of London that night. The following morning, 23 August, he was led on horseback to Westminster Hall in a procession which included his judges and the Lord Mayor of London. At his trial he was forced to wear a crown of laurel leaves in mockery. He removed it, but it was put back on his head.

His judges were Sir John De Segrave, Sir Peter Malory, the Lord Chief Justice, Ralph de Sandwich, the Constable of the Tower, John de Bacwell, a judge, and Sir John le Blound, the Lord Mayor of London. Wallace was charged with sedition, homicide, spoilation, robbery, arson and various other crimes. When charged with treason, Wallace managed to shout above the din that he could never be a traitor, as he had never recognised the King of England as his sovereign. We remember Wallace because he could never be bent; the English were determined to have him broken.

He was also charged with flying banners on the field of battle against the King of England. This would would have been the Lion Rampant, held by Scrymgeour, representing the sovereign of Scotland, or at least the sovereignty of Scotland, as the monarch was not present. But the ordinary soldiers of Scotland would have fought behind the St Andrew's cross, the Saltire of Scotland, the flag of the common people, and the oldest flag in the world. The Danes claim their flag is the oldest, and dates from the 1200s, but the blue and white flag of Scotland predates it by at least 400 years. The Scots have flown it since the battle of Athelstaneford, when a white cross appeared across the blue sky as an omen of victory. The white cross of St Andrew, backed by the blue of the sky, has been the banner of the ordinary Scot for well over a thousand years.

Westminster Hall is the oldest part of the Houses of Parliament. It was built by Rufus, son of William the Conqueror, in the late 1000s. In its day it was the largest free-standing building (ie, no pillars) in the world. To visit the Hall, you must apply to your local Member of Parliament for access to the Houses of Parliament. You pay a fee, and the guide allotted to you will give you a tour of the building, describing to you the greatness of English history in the passing. After going through the audience chambers, the House of Lords and the House of Commons, you are led into Westminster Hall. On the stairs is a plaque stating that this is the spot where Wallace was tried in 1305, near the King's Bench. I stood on this plaque and looked down the hall at the view that Wallace had seen 692 years before. It is hard to put my emotions at this time into words as I stood there so many years later, trying to feel how my fellow Scot had felt. I looked down the length of the hall to the great window, and gazed up at the mighty hammer-beam roof. All I could do was mouth that we were still here. The Scots are still here.

Wallace would have been struggling to keep his mind off

the horrors that lay ahead. He must have been hoping he could hold on to some sort of dignity through it all. But overriding all this would be his thoughts of Scotland which he would never see again. He must have despaired. Had he but known that Bruce would declare himself king only six months later. As far as Wallace was concerned, Scotland would die with him. Who was left to carry the flag? Had his life's work been a lost cause? He was dragged outside and tied to the tails of horses, probably wrapped in hide so that he would survive for the spectacle ahead. He was drawn from Westminster to the Tower of London, from the Tower to Aldgate, and through the heart of the city, to the elms at Smithfield.

Smithfield today is still a butchers' yard, and Wallace was taken there to be butchered. (Unlike *Braveheart*) there was no-one there for him in his hour of need. Each time he passed out, he would have been revived with cold water. He was hanged for the robberies, homicides and felonies he committed. Cut down alive, his genitals were cut off and burnt before him, because he was an outlaw to Edward of England. Because of his outrages against the Holy Church, his intestines were removed inch by inch. His ribcage was opened to show the gleeful audience his still beating heart, which was then torn out, ending his life. All his internal organs would then have been removed one by one, to be burnt, to dishonour him as much as possible. He was then beheaded, and his body dismembered.

There is a beautiful plaque on the wall of St Bartholomew's Hospital in King Street, overlooking Smithfield, and a group of elm trees that may be descended from those from Wallace's time. The plaque commemorates 'Sir William Wallace, patriot of Scotland, who was executed near this

Plaque at Smithfield

spot'. If you are ever in London, visit it, and take a few flowers to leave at its base. To one side of it stands the Church of St Bartholomew the Greater, the oldest church in London, founded in the same year as St Bartholomew's Hospital, 1123. It was to Wallace's right as he was executed, and so was one of the last things he saw, not that he would have taken it in. You can leave prayer cards here. You will know what you will write on yours if you ever visit. Mine said:

In memory of William Wallace
executed near here in the name of tyranny
murdered for the crime of treason that he did not commit.
We will not forget him.

At 10am on 23 August, 2005, God willing, I will walk from Westminster Hall to the Tower of London, from the Tower to Aldgate, then through the heart of the city to King Street at Smithfield, on the 700th anniversary of the day of Wallace's murder. It's the least I can do.

Menteith received £100 in land as his reward from

Newcastle

a grateful Edward. Wallace's head was fixed on London Bridge, and left there till it rotted and probably fell into the Thames below. This particular London Bridge survived until the 1600s. Sir John Segrave was granted 10 shillings for the carriage of the pieces of Wallace's body to Scotland. One quarter was hung on a gibbet at Newcastle, where Wallace had ravaged the surrounding countryside in his invasion of 1297-8. (MAP C6) Another quarter was sent to Berwick on Tweed. Wallace Green probably got its name from being the spot where his remains were exposed. A third quarter was taken to Stirling, probably hung from the bridge, the scene of his great victory, and the fourth was taken to St Johnstown of Perth, more than likely to be displayed above the town sewer. One English chronicle mentions Aberdeen as an alternative destination for part of Wallace's body, although there is nothing to substantiate this. Local legend has it that a star on the wall of the grounds of St. Nicholas Church in the town centre marks the burial place of one of Wallace's arms.

Edward believed that by mutilating Wallace, he was destroying him completely. He believed that the Scots would forget Wallace because of the manner of his death. Walter Bower, when writing the Scotichronicon in the 1440s, was profoundly aware of Edward's intentions regarding Wallace's execution. He makes several references to this; for example:

In the same year (1305) the noble William Wallace, suspecting no evil, was deceitfully and treacherously captured by Sir John de Menteith at Glasgow. He was handed over to the King of England and dismembered at London, and his limbs were hung up on towers in different places in England and Scotland to dishonour the Scots. By this that tyrant thought to destroy the fame of the noble Wallace for ever, since in the eyes of the foolish his life seemed to be ended with such a contemptible death.

700 years on, Wallace is a name revered in his native land and an inspiration to people in bondage the world over. I have seen letters from tribes in the rain forests of the Amazon who had somehow managed to view *Braveheart* and say that Wallace had given them the will to unite against those who were decimating their lands.

All we know of the route that William was 'drawn' through London was that he was taken from Westminster to the Tower of London, from there to the Aldgate, then through the heart of the city to Smithfield Elms, and his place of execution. At this time, Westminster stood well outside the walls of London. We know that on the eve of his 'trial', the crowds were so great that he could not be incarcerated in the Tower. Bearing this in mind, it is possible to plan a rough guide to the route by discounting side streets etc., assuming that the crowd would be too great to allow passage.

I am fairly sure, after studying medieval maps of London, that this route is fairly accurate, bar minor deviations. Many of the street names in London have existed for many centuries, many of them pre-dating Wallace's time. For example, Fleet Street takes its name from a stream of the same name that runs into the Thames, Aldgate tube station stands on the site of the original Aldgate, and Smithfield was always the city's meat market, although it stood outwith the town walls in the early 1300s. The main through routes follow the same basic directions as they did then, and it is obvious that Wallace would have been paraded down the

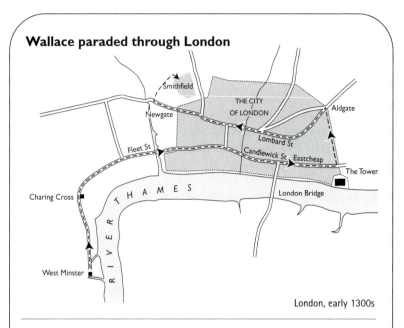

Wallace paraded through London

London, early 1300s

Modern Equivalent of Wallace's 'Drawing' through London

From the gate leading into Westminster Hall in the Houses of Parliament, turn right (north). Pass Parliament Square and into Parliament Street, which leads north into Whitehall. At Trafalgar Square turn north-east into The Strand. The route continues on through Fleet Street and on into Ludgate Hill. As you enter Ludgate Hill, this is the site of the Ludgate in the wall of the City of London, and where Wallace entered the city proper. At St Paul's Cathedral, you enter a thoroughfare named St Paul's Churchyard. This leads on into Cannon Street. Follow Cannon Street on to The Monument, then on into Eastcheap, continuing into Great Tower Street. You then reach Byward Street, which leads on to Tower Hill. You are now passing the Tower of London. A left turn is taken here, following the edge of the old city boundary, northwards up Minories to the Aldgate, another old gate of the city of London. Turning left here, take a right turn off Aldgate into Leadenhall Street. It was somewhere to the south of here that Wallace had been incarcerated the night before his trial, in the parish of St Gabriel's in Fenchurch Street. From Leadenhall Street continue on into Poultry, then on into Cheapside. This leads on to Newgate Street where Wallace was taken through the 'Newgate' out of the city. Turn right into Giltspur Street, following the side of St Bartholomew's Hospital to West Smithfield at Smithfield Market, and the plaque on the wall of St Barts.

main thoroughfares, so the spectacle could be watched by as many of the citizens as possible.

On the 700th anniversary of Stirling Bridge, Scotland began to take pride in shaping its destiny again. The Stone of Destiny has returned. Several Wallace marches take place on an annual basis. Andrew Murray is remembered for his uprising in the north. Where is Edward now?

CHAPTER 14

Edward's End

WE CANNOT FINISH THE story of William Wallace without following the fate of his great enemy, Edward of England. Edward's policy towards Scotland continued to his death. After Bruce declared himself king, some six months after Wallace's murder, many Scots threw off their allegiance to England, and again joined the national cause.

Sir Simon Fraser, Wallace's companion, joined Bruce, but was captured and taken to London where he was drawn and hung, and after his death he was beheaded, his head being mounted on a pole beside Wallace's on London Bridge. Alexander Scrymgeour, the standard bearer, was captured serving Bruce, and hung at Newcastle on 4 August, 1306. Edward's conduct towards the womenfolk of the Bruce family was shocking: he locked them up in cages that were hung over the walls of castles for all to gaze upon like animals in a zoo. He had Wallace's younger brother John drawn, hung and beheaded in London. His head probably joined Wallace's on London Bridge, so the passing populace could marvel at Edward's justice.

Edward spent the last six months of his life at Lanercost Abbey, where he could be close to Scotland in order to direct operations. (MAP C4) The guest house where he resided is still occupied as a church building. But his health was fading. Bruce's continuing success in evading capture, then his successes against the English forces, prompted Edward to muster yet another army to subjugate Scotland. He had to be

126

carried on a litter, but rested at Carlisle, only ten miles from Lanercost, as he was beginning to fail. (MAP C3) When news of Bruce's victory at Glen Trool reached him, he declared himself fit and donated his litter to Carlisle Cathedral. One can only marvel at his determination to conquer Scotland, a determination that lasted to the bitter end.

He marched his army north-west to the edge of the Solway. Invading armies would come this way to cross the sands of the estuary at low tide which made more sense than trying to go via Gretna, where the ground was very boggy, with poor footing for horses. Crossing by the sands, the English would arrive on Scottish soil near Annan, then continue straight on up Annandale. Just north of Burgh on Sands, Edward had a seizure and knew his end had come. (MAP C2) Legend states that he called his son, the future Edward II, to his tent where he commanded him that after his death he was to boil his body in a cauldron till the flesh came away from the bones. The flesh could be discarded, but his bones were to be carried in front of the army till the last Scots were crushed underfoot.

Edward II was a different kettle of fish from his father. He had Longshanks' body taken south to Westminster Abbey for burial. In preparation for the journey, the entrails, brain and intestines were removed from the body and buried at the abbey of Holm Cultram in Abbeytown, some 18 miles south-west of Carlisle. (MAP C1) Organs were removed from the dead in those days as a simple necessity, since bodies would start to decay on long journeys.

Holm Cultram Abbey

The Scotichronicon states, 'In Burgh-by-Sands where the borders of the kingdom end, Edward died who evilly killed Scots. His entrails were buried with his brain at Holm'. Holm Cultram is also the last resting place of the father of Robert the Bruce, who died in 1304. His gravestone stands upright in the later porch of the abbey.

Burgh on Sands

Edward II did advance into Scotland, but after reaching Cumnock in Ayrshire, he turned back without achieving anything.

The spot on the grassland on the Solway where Edward died on 7 July, 1307, aged 69, is marked by a pillar surrounded by an iron railing. It stands a mile or so north of Burgh on Sands. This village had been a station post during the days of the Roman occupation, and the stones from it were used to build St Michael's church. Taking the farm road north from the village, you can park where the road splits, and

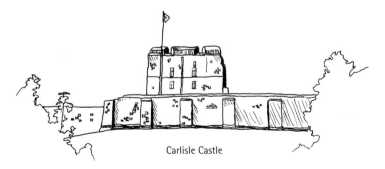

Carlisle Castle

walk the last several hundred yards to the monument. It is a desolate spot on a windy rainy day, but quite transformed in the summer, with the skylarks rising, trilling into the sky. It is a place for contemplation. It is strange to imagine a huge army waiting there, idle, motionless, while their king breathed his last. The view across the Solway to Scotland is the same as Edward saw as he died cursing that perfidious northern race.

The cathedral and the castle in Carlisle, where so many Scots met their end over the centuries, are worth visiting, as is Lanercost Abbey which Wallace and Edward knew well.

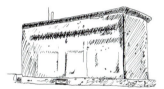

Edwards Tomb

Edward lies in Westminster Abbey, his plain stone tomb standing in the chapel of Edward the Confessor. A later hand has inscribed on the side of his last resting place:

Edwardus Primus. Malletus Scotorum Rex. Pactum Serva,

or

Edward the First. Hammer of the Scots. Keep Faith.

Hammer he may have been, but every time he went back south across the border, the Scots rebelled again. He may have marched over Scottish land, but he never reigned over it.

Others who took part in the Wars of Independence are entombed in Westminster, most notably Aymer de Valance.

It is a quirk of history that Wallace must have seen what was to be Edward's last resting place. When he was taken to Westminster Hall he would have been able to see Westminster Abbey close by. It had by then already become the resting place of the Stone of Destiny.

Edward may have a marble tomb in the heart of London as his memorial, whereas Wallace's body was scattered to the four winds, but Wallace's greatest epitaph is in the hearts of the people of Scotland, who will remember him till the ends of time. Many historical heroes have their flaws, and Wallace surely had his, but it is for his purity of purpose, the steadfastness of his resolve, and his unshakeable love of his native soil that each successive generation of Scots remembers him.

CHAPTER 15

Wallace Connections at Home and Abroad

THIS BOOK WAS NEVER meant to be a history book. Other writers have done justice to the historical side of Wallace. I have tried to do it differently by making this not only the story of Wallace's life, but a rough guide to sites that are associated with him. There are some places, however, that have a Wallace name or a tenuous connection, which for one reason or another I have not been able to weave into the story. There will also be places which people connect in their local area with Wallace that have never come to my attention, and if any appear to be glaring omissions, I apologise. There are even Wallace sites abroad, where expatriate Scots or admirers of Wallace have commemorated his life in some way.

Between the road from Blantyre to Uddingston and the River Clyde, high on a crag directly opposite Bothwell Castle, is the site of Blantyre Priory. This priory was founded by Alexander II in the 1200s. It has almost entirely disappeared, and only the trace of an outline of walls survives. But in the 1800s, two red sandstone gables and a vault were still standing from this once impressive building, and a window in one of the gables was for many years pointed out as being the one through which Wallace escaped when English soldiers burst into the building. He jumped through it to the wooded crags below and got away. Below the priory site there are some life-size carvings of the crucifiction on the cliff-face. I have never been able to ascertain the age of these carvings.

Perhaps they date back to the days when monks were in residence at the priory above, but they are weather worn, being carved in soft sandstone, and I would not like to hazard a guess as to their age.

Bothwell Castle is a monument to the power of the Murrays who built it. It would have been the latest in feudal magnificence when Wallace was alive, and as many of his exploits took place on the banks of the Clyde, he would have known it. Bothwell Castle is open to the public, and is signposted from the centre of Uddingston.

In upper Clydesdale, five or six miles south-east of Lanark, near the village of Thankerton, stands a curiously symmetrical hill by the name of Quothquan. (MAP B11) It is 1,097ft high, and even at a distance you can see the ancient earthworks around the summit. The haul to the top is worth it if only for the view across the Clyde to Tinto. I have seen a couple of references to a rock outcrop on the summit which bears the name Wallace's Chair. As the hill stands midway between Lanark and Lamington, Wallace was probably quite familiar with the location.

Above the east end of Port Glasgow stands Devol's Glen. At the head of this glen is a precipice called Wallace's Leap, over which Wallace is fabled to have leapt on horseback.

One mile west of the town of Dumbarton, in a red sandstone cliff, is Wallace's Cave. In the 17th century it was known simply as the Hole of Havock.

Apart from the famous Wallace Oak at Elderslie, there were other oaks associated with Wallace. Near Torwood Castle in the wood of the same name, stood a noted Wallace Oak, a shoot of which survived till 1835. Even the roots of this tree were dug up to make Wallace momentoes. Part of the tree was used to make a presentation box for George

Washington. Another Wallace Oak stood at Kirkfieldbank on the Clyde below Lanark. Blind Harry makes several references to Kirkfieldbank, which he calls Kilbank or Gilbank in his narrative. (MAP B13)

If anyone has any doubt regarding the length of time that oaks can flourish, you need only visit Chatelherault near Hamilton. David I planted a wood of oaks there that have become contorted into amazing shapes. In winter they look like a bizarre throw-back to prehistoric days, but are reborn each year in a riot of summer greenery.

Kinnoull Hill, which soars above the Tay east of Perth, is a site with a possible Wallace connection. An old guide book describes it as follows:

> From Perth its summit is gained by a winding carriage-road, called Montagu's Walk after the Duke of Montagu, who was in Scotland when it was formed, and that summit commands a magnificent prospect, by Pennant entitled 'The glory of Scotland'. Near the Windy Gowl, a steep and hollow descent betwixt two tops of the hill, is a nine-times-repeating echo, and on the hill-face is the Dragon Hole, a cave where Wallace is said to have lain concealed, and where Beltane fires formerly were kindled.

St Margaret's Chapel in Edinburgh Castle is the oldest surviving building in Edinburgh. This tiny building stands on the highest point of the castle rock. (MAP A5) It contains a beautiful stained glass window of Wallace. Surprisingly, it is the only window which is not of a saint, which shows Wallace's importance in the soul of the nation. Famous statues of Wallace and Bruce flank the main entrance to the castle, now home to the Stone of Destiny – not a popular decision with many Scots, as the castle is a British Army barracks. When it was announced that the Stone was being returned, a popular rhyme was coined:

> Scone for the purists
> Edinburgh for the tourists.

Little couplets like this are like an echo from the old chronicles.

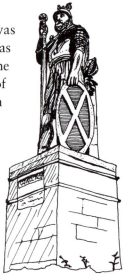

A tower in Edinburgh Castle was known as the Wallace Tower, but it was reduced to rubble in 1573 during the thirty-three days' seige by the troops of Regent Morton and the English auxiliaries under Sir William Drury. A spot on the north-facing cliff of the castle rock is known as Wallace's Cradle.

Near Corses Cottages in Dumfriesshire stand the 'six corses' – stones that supposedly mark where some English dead were buried after an encounter with Wallace.

Wallace Statue, Dryburgh

The first monument to be raised to Wallace in Scotland was the sandstone giant which stands on a hillside above Dryburgh Abbey on the Tweed. (MAP C12) It was erected by the eleventh Earl of Buchan who was very attached to the Dryburgh area and was buried in the Abbey. He built a 260-foot suspension bridge over the Tweed, and commissioned John Smith, a sculptor, to design the Wallace statue. He copied its likeness from a supposedly authentic portrait of Wallace which had been purchased in France by Sir Philip Ainslie of Pilton.

There are several of these so-called authentic portraits of Wallace in existence. They all show a heavy, bearded man who appears to be around 55 years of age, wearing a helmet with what looks like a dragon mounted on top. As Wallace was only in his early to mid twenties at the height of his career, doubt is cast on these images immediately.

The statue at Dryburgh, 21.5 ft high, was placed on its plinth in September 1814. It was originally painted white, and the writer, Chambers, commented, 'It occupies so eminent a situation that this statue of Wallace, frowning towards England, is visible even from Berwick, a distance of more than 30 miles'. Certainly, on its large plinth, I have seen many visitors taken aback at its enormity. At the time of writing, a small box stood to the left of the statue, in which people could leave notes. Most of them are brief patriotic statements, with many foreigners writing 'Freedom', etc. A sandstone urn stands right in front of the statue, bearing what old accounts describe as 'a suitable inscription' of the story of Wallace, but due to erosion it has become ever more illegible over time. The statue was restored around 1990.

Occasionally I come across references in old books to places with a Wallace connection, some of which I have not visited and so cannot say whether the sites still exist. One such example is as follows, taken from the Ordnance Gazetteer of Scotland of the 1890s:

Ditch Hall – an ancient structure of earth and turf on Inverchadain farm, in Fortingal Parish, Perthshire. It is described by Blind Harry, is said to have been Sir

William Wallace's resting place for a few days, and the place where he was joined by the men of Rannoch, on the eve of his march against the English at Dunkeld and Perth, and is still represented by some remains.

More surprising, however, are the Wallace sites abroad. In the goldfields of Ballarat in Australia stands a statue of Wallace. It was commissioned by the Caledonian Society there, and bequeathed to the public of Ballarat by James Russell Thomson. The statue, which was unveiled on 24 May, 1898, was sculpted by Percival Ball of Melbourne, who used as his model the famous Scottish World Champion athlete, Donald Dinnie (1837 – 1916), whose muscular form was to grace the labels on the Scottish soft drink 'Barrs Irn Bru' for many years.

In New Jersey in the USA, is a glen dedicated to the memory of our hero. The signs as you enter the glen state:

The Wallace Glen,
Dedicated to Sir William Wallace, the great Scottish patriot and hero, who fought for freedom for his countrymen, and gave his life in this noble cause.

One of the most amazing memorials for me is the statue of Wallace in Druid Hill Park in the city of Baltimore. This statue is a copy of the one that graces the National Wallace Monument at Stirling. It was erected by the local St Andrew's Society in 1893. The statue is 13ft high, made of black iron, and is set above a high stone plinth which bears the legend:

Wallace, patriot and martyr for Scottish liberty, 1305.

The local newspaper carried the following account in 1893:

12,000 people were gathered around the colossal statue and they gave a mighty cheer when the veil which hid the massive beauty of the statue fell away, leaving it sharply outlined against the clear winter sky.

In presenting the statue to the city, the principal donor, Mr William Wallace Spence, stated:

Although centuries have passed since Wallace fought and died for Scotland, his name is still cherished deep down in the hearts of his countrymen as one of the noblest and grandest on the pages of history. It was this man who, by his precept and example, implanted in Scotland that indomitable and inextinguishable love of freedom which has been a distinguishing characteristic of Scotchmen in every quarter of the globe. This was abundantly manifested by them in this, their adopted country, for which they so freely shed their blood in the trying days of the American Revolution.

CHAPTER 16

Wallace through the Ages

THE LEGEND OF WALLACE has continually re-invented itself.
John of Fordun's chronicle says of Wallace:

> He was wondrously brave and bold of goodly mien,
> and boundless liberality, and though, among the earls
> and lords of the kingdom, he was looked upon as
> low-born, yet his fathers rejoiced in the honour of
> knighthood. His elder brother, also, was girded with
> the knightly belt, and inherited a landed estate which
> was large enough for his station...

By the time of the Scotichronicon in the 1440s, he was
described as:

> A tall man with the body of a giant, cheerful in
> appearance with agreeable features, broad shouldered
> and big boned, with belly in proportion and lengthy
> flanks, pleasing in appearance but with a wild look,
> broad in the hips with strong arms and legs, a most
> spirited fighting man...

> Fair in his judgements, most compassionate in com-
> forting the sad, a most skilful counsellor, very patient
> when suffering, a distinguished speaker, who above all
> hunted down falsehood and deceit and detested
> treachery, for this reason the Lord was with him.

English chroniclers are all equally damning of Wallace, describing him as a 'brigand', 'thief', 'master of thieves', etc. The Lanercost chronicle describes his death thus:

> The vilest doom is fittest for thy crimes
> Justice demands that thou should die three times.
> Thou pillager of many a sacred shrine,
> Butcher of thousands, threefold death be thine!
> So shall the English from thee gain relief
> Scotland! be wise and choose a nobler chief

The main source for legends regarding Wallace being the work of Blind Harry, Harry mentions in his poem that he had access to a work on Wallace written by John Blair, Wallace's personal chaplain. After Wallace's murder, Blair supposedly wrote a biography of his life, commissioned by Bishop Sinclair of Dunkeld. This book is lost to us, and historians have called into question whether Blair ever actually existed.

The history of Dunfermline Abbey by the Rev J M Webster contains the following:

> Arnald (alias John) Blair. Born in the county of Fife, in the reign of Alexander III, and educated with Sir William Wallace at the school of Dundee, he went to France, studied at Paris, and entered into holy orders. On his return to Scotland, he retired to the Benedictine cloister of Dunfermline. But when Sir William Wallace was made governor or viceroy of the Kingdom in 1297, he was called out of the monastery and made his chaplain, and being an eye-witness of most of his actions, he composed the history of his life in Latin...

It is a pity that this story cannot be accepted unreservedly. It is not seriously questioned that John Blair may have acted as chaplain to Sir William Wallace and written the story of his life. There is, moreover, documentary evidence that three sons of Sir Alexander de Blair, Adam, David and George, were members of the monastery of Dunfermline c. 1278.

Thinking about this 'lost' book by Blair reminds me of the Prayer Book of St Margaret, Queen of Scots and wife of Malcolm Canmore, the whereabouts of which were unknown for 800 years. It then turned up at a book sale and is now in the Bodleian Library in Oxford.

Blind Harry composed his poem to recite at various lordly establishments throughout Scotland, where he would be paid in food, lodgings and clothing. His work was written down around 1477, and was first printed by Chepman and Myllar around 1508. It ran to 23 editions. In 1722 it was translated into a more modern version by William Hamilton of Gilbertfield, and this edition inspired Burns among others. The ruins of Gilbertfield still stand and lie between Cathkin, on the southern outskirts of Glasgow, and Dechmont Hill. Gilbertfield is an 'L-plan' tower house, most of which is complete to the wallhead, although one wing has collapsed in recent years.

The historian, Hector Boece, described how King James the First visited an old lady near Kinnoul in Perthshire who had seen and remembered both Wallace and Bruce. She said Robert was of eminent beauty and strength, but in the latter quality was excelled by Wallace. This is a nice little story, but the lady would have had to have been around 120 years old to have remembered them.

There is an interesting description of Bruce by John Mair in his *Historia Majoris Britanniae*:

His figure was graceful and atheltic, with broad

shoulders, his features were handsome, he had the yellow hair of the northern race, with blue and sparkling eyes. His intellect was quick, and he had the gift of fluent speech in the vernacular, delightful to listen to.

Unfortunately, nothing so straightforward exists to describe Wallace. Most accounts of his appearance mention that he had a large scar on his neck, the legacy of an arrow wound.

The story of Wallace carried on through the medium of speech and eventually the printed word, adapting itself always for the audience of the day. The use of cinema to tell his story was inevitable. The writer of *Braveheart*, Randall Wallace, was aware that his name had a Scottish origin. The following are remarks by him that I have picked up from conversations and from a speech he made to an audience of *Braveheart* afficionados. He used to tease his wife, telling her that 'We Wallaces are really big in Scotland'. When he eventually came to the 'old country' on holiday, one of the obvious things to do as a tourist was visit Edinburgh Castle. As he went through the gate he noticed the statue of Wallace on one side, and jokingly remarked to his wife, 'Look, I told you we Wallaces were big in Scotland!' Entering the castle, he asked a guard who this famous Wallace was. The guard replied, 'That, sir, is our greatest hero!'

When he got back to Los Angeles, he decided to find out more. The UCLA library produced some works on Wallace, but they were in Latin. I can only guess that they were from an old chronicle. Randall informed them that this was no good to him. Several days later the library telephoned to say they had found another work in deep storage, ie, something that no-one had expressed any interest in for many years. In fact, it is believed that it was due to be sent to the incinerator. It turned out to be a Hamilton of Gilbertfield edition of *Blind Harry*. Randall absorbed every detail, and *Braveheart* was scripted from Blind Harry's work.

Braveheart received some scathing comments from the press regarding its inaccuracies, many of which were part and parcel of Harry's work. But Harry wrote his work to be entertainment, and a spur to Scots to feel patriotism for their native soil. *Braveheart* is certainly entertainment, having won five Oscars, and it certainly stirred patriotic feelings in most Scots, but it was a catalyst for the huge increase in sales of Scottish history books. If people are taking a pride in their heritage, it cannot be a bad thing; after all, how do you know your destination if you don't know where you have travelled from? Nigel Tranter, the famous Scots author, once said that most Scots are like a man who has lost his memory, groping blindly on, with no idea as to his past. If *Braveheart* has gone even a small way towards rectifying this situation, then it has to be a good thing.

Many people picked up on the fact that in the film there was no bridge in the Battle of Stirling. Seoras Wallace from Glasgow, whose organisation, the Wallace Clan, was in the forefront of many of the battle scenes, mentioned that he was glad there was no bridge, since there could have been fatalities with so many of his compatriots putting their all into the fight scenes.

No matter what, the film will stand for all time to show how Wallace was perceived in 1995. No doubt the time will come when it will look as dated as early black and white films appear to us today. But it is another part of the continuing Wallace story, and I have no doubt that new bits and pieces will come to light to enable the story to continue.

Scotland is lucky to have such a champion. No matter what the future holds politically, or how low Scotland's fortunes may sink, Wallace will always be there as an example for men and women never to give up hope, despite horrendous odds. Wallace, one man, gave all he had for his country. In time to come, one like-minded soul may be all that is needed to ensure that Scotland will have a future, even if, like Wallace, he may think that Scotland ends with him.

I would like to finish by quoting from A F Murison's book, *Sir William Wallace*, published in 1898:

To the memory of the comrades and helpers of Sir William Wallace,
Men or Women, distinguished, obscure or nameless.

Bibliography

Chronicles of the Crusades (Bramley Books, Surrey, 1997)

Ordnance Gazetteer of Scotland (William MacKenzie, London, 1893)

The Topographical, Statistical and Historical Gazetteer of Scotland (A. Fullarton & Co., Glasgow, 1842)

BARROW, G.W.S   Kingship and Unity : Scotland 1000 – 1306 (Edward Arnold, London, 1981)

BARROW, G.W.S   Robert Bruce (Edinburgh University Press, Third Edition, Edinburgh, 1988)

BINGHAM, Caroline   The Kings and Queens of Scotland (Weidenfeld and Nicolson, London, 1976)

BOWER, Walter   Scotichronicon, Edited by D.E.R. Watt (Aberdeen University Press, 1991)

FERGUSSON, James   William Wallace, Guardian of Scotland (Alexander MacLehose & Co., Edinburgh, 1938)

FISHER, Andrew   William Wallace (John Donald, Edinburgh, 1986)

FORDUN, John   Chronicle of the Scottish Nation, Edited by W.F. Skene (Edmonston and Douglas, 1872)

GRAY, D.J.   William Wallace – The King's Enemy
                                (Hale Ltd., London, 1991)

HAMILTON, William,   Blind Harry's Wallace
of Gilbertfield   (Luath Press, Edinburgh, 1998)

HENDRIE, William F.   Linlithgow, Six Hundred Years a Royal
                                Burgh (John Donald, Edinburgh, 1989)

HOWELL, Rev. A.R.   Paisley Abbey
                                (Alexander Gardner Ltd, Paisley, 1929)

KING, Elspeth   Introducing William Wallace
                                (The Scottish Collection by Firtree
                                Publishing, Forth William, 1997)

MACFARLANE, Walter   Geographical Collections Relating to
                                Scotland
                                (University Press, Edinburgh, 1907)

MACKAY, James   William Wallace, Brave Heart
                                (Mainstream, Edinburgh, 1995)

MACPHAIL, I.M.M.   Dumbarton Castle
                                (John Donald, 1979)

MURISON, A. F.   Sir William Wallace
                                (Famous Scots Series, Oliphant, Anderson
                                & Ferrier, Edinburgh, 1898)

PREBBLE, John   The Lion in the North
                                (Robert MacLehose & Co, Glasgow, 1974)

PRESTWICH, Michael   Edward 1
                                (Yale English Monarchs, Methven, London,
                                1997)

REESE, Peter   Wallace, A Biography
                                (Canongate, Edinburgh, 1996)

SALTER, Mike   The Castles of Scotland Series, Five
                      Volumes (Folly Publications, Worcester,
                      1994)

TURNBULL, Michael   Saint Andrew
                      (St Andrew Press, Edinburgh, 1997)

WEBSTER, Rev. J.M.   Dunfermline Abbey
                      (The Carnegie Dunfermline Trust,
                      Dunfermline, 1948)

WILSON, Alan J.   St. Margaret, Queen of Scotland
                      (John Donald, Edinburgh, 1993)

Some other books published by **LUATH** PRESS

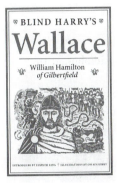

Blind Harry's Wallace

William Hamilton of Gilbertfield

ISBN 0 946487 43 X HBK £15.00
ISBN 0 946487 33 2 PBK £8.99

The original story of the real braveheart, Sir William Wallace. Racy, blood on every page, violently anglophobic, grossly embellished, vulgar and disgusting, clumsy and stilted, a literary failure, a great epic.

Whatever the verdict on BLIND HARRY, this is the book which has done more than any other to frame the notion of Scotland's national identity. Despite its numerous 'historical inaccuracies', it remains the principal source for what we now know about the life of Wallace.

The novel and film *Braveheart* were based on the 1722 Hamilton edition of this epic poem. Burns, Wordsworth, Byron and others were greatly influenced by this version 'wherein the old obsolete words are rendered more intelligible', which is said to be the book, next to the Bible, most commonly found in Scottish households in the eighteenth century. Burns even admits to having 'borrowed... a couplet worthy of Homer' directly from Hamilton's version of BLIND HARRY to include in *Scots wha hae.*

Elspeth King, in her introduction to this, the first accessible edition of BLIND HARRY in verse form since 1859, draws parallels between the situation in Scotland at the time of Wallace and that in Bosnia and Chechnya in the 1990s. Seven hundred years to the day after the Battle of Stirling Bridge, the 'Settled Will of the Scottish People' was expressed in the devolution referendum of 11 September 1997. She describes this as a landmark opportunity for mature reflection on how the nation has been shaped, and sees BLIND HARRY'S WALLACE as an essential and compelling text for this purpose.

'Builder of the literary foundations of a national hero-cult in a free and powerful country'.

ALEXANDER STODDART, sculptor

'A true bard of the people'

TOM SCOTT, THE PENGUIN BOOK OF SCOTTISH VERSE, on Blind Harry.

'A more inventive writer than Shakespeare'

RANDALL WALLACE

'The story of Wallace poured a Scottish prejudice in my veins which will boil along until the floodgates of life shut in eternal rest'.

ROBERT BURNS

'Hamilton's couplets are not the best poetry you will ever read, but they rattle along at a fair pace. In re-issuing this work, the publishers have re-opened the spring from which most of our conceptions of the Wallace legend come'.

SCOTLAND ON SUNDAY

'The return of Blind Harry's Wallace, a man who makes Mel look like a wimp'.

THE SCOTSMAN

Notes from the North
incorporating a Brief History of the Scots and the English
Emma Wood

ISBN 0 946487 46 4 PBK £8.99

Notes on being English
Notes on being in Scotland
Learning from a shared past

Is it time to recognise that the border between Scotland and England is the dividing line between very different cultures?

As the Scottish nation begins to set its own agenda, will it decide to consign its sense of grievance against England to the dustbin of history?

Will a fresh approach heal these ancient 'sibling rivalries'?

How does a study of Scottish history help to clarify the roots of Scottish-English antagonism?

Does an English 'white settler' have a right to contribute to the debate?

Will the empowering of the citizens of Scotland take us all, Scots and English, towards mutual tolerance and understanding?

Sickened by the English jingoism that surfaced in rampant form during the 1982 Falklands War, Emma Wood started to dream of moving from her home in East Anglia to the Highlands of Scotland. She felt increasingly frustrated and marginalised as Thatcherism got a grip on the southern English psyche. The Scots she met on frequent holidays in the Highlands had no truck with Thatcherism, and she felt at home with grass-roots Scottish anti-authoritarianism. The decision was made. She uprooted and headed for a new life in the north of Scotland.

She was to discover that she had crossed a border in more than the geographical sense.

Loving her new life and friends in first Sutherland and then Ross-shire, she nevertheless had to come to terms with the realisation that in the eyes of some Scots she was an unwelcome 'white settler' who would never belong. She became aware of the perception that some English incomers were insensitive to the needs and aspirations of Highland communities.

Her own approach has been thoughtful and creative. In *Notes from the North* she sets a study of Scots-English conflicts alongside relevant personal experiences of contemporary incomers' lives in the Highlands. She gently and perceptively confronts the issue of racial intolerance, and sets out conflicting perceptions of 'Englishness' and 'Scottishness'; she argues that racial stereotyping is a stultifying cul-de-sac, and that distinctive ethnic and cultural strands within Scottish society are potentially enriching and strengthening forces. This book is a pragmatic, positive and forward-looking contribution to cultural and politicial debate within Scotland.

Notes from the North is essential reading for anyone who is thinking of moving to Scotland and for Scots who want to move into the 21st century free of unnecessary baggage from the past.

The Bannockburn Years
William Scott

ISBN 0 946487 34 0 PBK £7.95

A present day Edinburgh solicitor stumbles across reference to a document of value to the Nation State of Scotland. He tracks down the document on the Isle of Bute, a document which probes the real 'quaestiones' about nationhood and national identity. The document ends up being published, but is it authentic and does it matter? Almost 700 years on, these 'quaestiones' are still worth asking.

Written with pace and passion, William Scott has devised an intriguing vehicle to open up new ways of looking at the future of Scotland and its people. He presents an alternative interpretation of how the Battle of Bannockburn was fought, and through the Bannatyne manuscript he draws the reader into the minds of those involved.

Winner of the 1997 Constable Trophy, the premier award in Scotland for an unpublished novel, this book offers new insights to both the academic and the general reader which are sure to provoke further discussion and debate.

'A brilliant storyteller. I shall expect to see your name writ large hereafter.'
NIGEL TRANTER, October 1997

'... a compulsive read.' PH SCOTT, *The Scotsman*

Old Scotland New Scotland
Jeff Fallow

ISBN 0 946487 40 5 PBK £6.99

'Together we can build a new Scotland based on Labour's values.' DONALD DEWAR, Party Political Broadcast

'Despite the efforts of decent Mr Dewar, the voters may yet conclude they are looking at the same old hacks in brand new suits.' IAN BELL, *The Independent*

'At times like this you suddenly realise how dangerous the neglect of Scottish history in our schools and universities may turn out to be.' MICHAEL FRY, *The Herald*

'...one of the things I hope will go is our chip on the shoulder about the English... The SNP has a huge responsibility to articulate Scottish independence in a way that is pro-Scottish and not anti-English.' ALEX SALMOND, *The Scotsman*

Scottish politics have never been more exciting. In *old Scotland new Scotland* Jeff Fallow takes us on a graphic voyage through Scotland's turbulent history, from earliest times through to the present day and beyond. This fast-track guide is the quick way to learn what your history teacher didn't tell you, essential reading for all who seek an understanding of Scotland and its history.

Eschewing the romanticisation of his country's past, Fallow offers a new perspective on an old nation. 'Too many people associate Scottish history with tartan trivia or outworn romantic myth. This book aims to blast that stubborn idea.' JEFF FALLOW

An Inhabited Solitude: Scotland – Land and People

James McCarthy

ISBN 0 946487 30 8 PBK £6.99

'*Scotland is the country above all others that I have seen, in which a man of imagination may carve out his own pleasures; there are so many inhabited solitudes.*'

DOROTHY WORDSWORTH, in her journal of August 1803

An informed and thought-provoking profile of Scotland's unique landscapes and the impact of humans on what we see now and in the future. James McCarthy leads us through the many aspects of the land and the people who inhabit it: natural Scotland; the rocks beneath; land ownership; the use of resources; people and place; conserving Scotland's heritage and much more.

Written in a highly readable style, this concise volume offers an understanding of the land as a whole. Emphasising the uniqueness of the Scottish environment, the author explores the links between this and other aspects of our culture as a key element in rediscovering a modern sense of the Scottish identity and perception of nationhood.

'*This book provides an engaging introduction to the mysteries of Scotland's people and landscapes. Difficult concepts are described in simple terms, providing the interested Scot or tourist with an invaluable overview of the country... It fills an important niche which, to my knowledge, is filled by no other publications.*'

BETSY KING, Chief Executive, Scottish Environmental Education Council.

Over the Top with the Tartan Army (Active Service 1992-97)

Andrew McArthur

ISBN 0 946487 45 6 PBK £7.99

Scotland has witnessed the growth of a new and curious military phenomenon – grown men bedecked in tartan yomping across the globe, hell-bent on benevolence and ritualistic bevvying. What noble cause does this famous army serve? Why, football of course!

Taking us on an erratic world tour, McArthur gives a frighteningly funny insider's eye view of active service with the Tartan Army – the madcap antics of Scotland's travelling support in the '90s, written from the inside, covering campaigns and skirmishes from Euro '92 up to the qualifying drama for France '98 in places as diverse as Russia, the Faroes, Belarus, Sweden, Monte Carlo, Estonia, Latvia, USA and Finland.

This book is a must for any football fan who likes a good laugh.

'*I commend this book to all football supporters*'. GRAHAM SPIERS, *Scotland on Sunday*

'*In wishing Andy McArthur all the best with this publication, I do hope he will be in a position to produce a sequel after our participation in the World Cup in France*'. CRAIG BROWN, Scotland Team Coach

All royalties on sales of the book are going to Scottish charities, principally Children's Hospice Association Scotland, the only Scotland-wide charity of its kind, providing special love and care to children with terminal illnesses at its hospice, Rachel House, in Kinross.

A Word for Scotland

Jack Campbell
with a foreword by Magnus Magnusson
ISBN 0 946487 48 0 PBK £12.99

The inside story of a newspaper and a nation
– five tumultuous decades as they happened.

'A word for Scotland' was Lord Beaverbrook's hope when he founded the *Scottish Daily Express*. That word for Scotland quickly became, and was for many years, the national newspaper of Scotland.

The pages of *A Word For Scotland* exude warmth and a wry sense of humour. Jack Campbell takes us behind the scenes to meet the larger-than-life characters and ordinary people who made and recorded the stories. Here we hear the stories behind the stories that hit the headlines in this great yarn of journalism in action.

Jack joined the infant newspaper at the age of 15 as a copy-boy. The young lad from Govan went on to become a leading player through nearly half a century of the most exciting, innovative and competitive years of the press in Scotland, finishing up as managing editor. He remembers the early days of news-gathering on a shoestring, the circulation wars, all the scoops and dramas and tragedies through nearly half a century of the most exciting, innovative and competitive years of the press in Scotland. He was with the *Scottish Daily Express* through the dramatic events of 1974 which ended the paper's long reign at 195 Albion Street, Glasgow.

It would be true to say 'all life is here'. From the Cheapside Street fire of which cost the lives of 19 Glasgow firemen, to the theft of the Stone of Destiny, to the lurid exploits of serial killer Peter Manuel, to encounters with world boxing champions Benny Lynch and Cassius Clay – this book offers telling glimpses of the characters, events, joy and tragedy which make up Scotland's story in the 20th century.

'*As a rookie reporter you were proud to work on it and proud to be part of it - it was fine newspaper right at the heartbeat of Scotland.*'

RONALD NEIL, Chief Executive of BBC Production, and a reporter on the *Scottish Daily Express* (1963-68)

'*This book is a fascinating reminder of Scottish*

journalism in its heyday. It will be read avidly by those journalists who take pride in their profession – and should be compulsory reading for those who don't.'

JACK WEBSTER, columnist on *The Herald* and *Scottish Daily Express* journalist (1960-80)

LUATH GUIDES TO SCOTLAND

Highways and Byways in Mull and Iona

Peter Macnab
ISBN 0 946487 16 2 PBK £4.25

Southwest Scotland

Tom Atkinson
ISBN 0 946487 04 9 PBK £4.95

The Lonely Lands

Tom Atkinson
ISBN 0 946487 10 3 PBK £4.95

The Empty Lands

Tom Atkinson
ISBN 0 946487 13 8 PBK £4.95

Roads to the Isles

Tom Atkinson
ISBN 0 946487 01 4 PBK £4.95

NATURAL SCOTLAND

Wild Scotland: the essential guide to finding the best of natural Scotland

James McCarthy
Photography by Laurie Campbell
ISBN 0 946487 37 5 PBK £7.50

Rum: Nature's Island

Magnus Magnusson
ISBN 0 946487 32 4 PBK £7.95

The Highland Geology Trail

John L Roberts
ISBN 0 946487 36 7 PBK £4.99

FOLKLORE

Tall Tales from an Island

Peter Macnab
ISBN 0 946487 07 3 PBK £8.99

The Supernatural Highlands
Francis Thompson
ISBN 0 946487 31 6 PBK £8.99

WALK WITH LUATH

Mountain Days & Bothy Nights
Dave Brown and Ian Mitchell
ISBN 0 946487 15 4 PBK £7.50

The Joy of Hillwalking
Ralph Storer
ISBN 0 946487 28 6 PBK £7.50

Scotland's Mountains before the Mountaineers
Ian Mitchell
ISBN 0 946487 39 1 PBK £9.99

LUATH WALKING GUIDES

Walks in the Cairngorms
Ernest Cross
ISBN 0 946487 09 X PBK £3.95

Short Walks in the Cairngorms
Ernest Cross
ISBN 0 946487 23 5 PBK £3.95

SPORT

Ski & Snowboard Scotland
Hilary Parke
ISBN 0 946487 35 9 PBK £6.99

SOCIAL HISTORY

The Crofting Years
Francis Thompson
ISBN 0 946487 06 5 PBK £6.95

MUSIC AND DANCE

Highland Balls and Village Halls
GW Lockhart
ISBN 0 946487 12 X PBK £6.95

Fiddles & Folk: a celebration of the re-emergence of Scotland's musical heritage
GW Lockhart
ISBN 0 946487 38 3 PBK £7.95

FICTION

The Great Melnikov
Hugh MacLachlan
ISBN 0 946487 42 1 PBK £7.95

BIOGRAPHY

Tobermory Teuchter: a first-hand account of life on Mull in the early years of the 20th century
Peter Macnab
ISBN 0 946487 41 3 PBK £7.99

Bare Feet and Tackety Boots
Archie Cameron
ISBN 0 946487 17 0 PBK £7.95

Come Dungeons Dark
John Taylor Caldwell
ISBN 0 946487 19 7 PBK £6.95

POETRY

Poems to be read aloud
Collected and with an introduction by Tom Atkinson
ISBN 0 946487 00 6 PBK £5.00

COMING SOON...

On the Trail of Robert the Bruce
David R. Ross
ISBN 0 946487 52 9 PBK £7.99

On the Trail of Mary Queen of Scots
J. Keith Cheetham
ISBN 0 946487 50 2 PBK £7.99

On the Trail of Robert Service
G Wallace Lockhart
ISBN 0 946487 24 3 PBK £7.99

On the Trail of Robert Burns
John Cairney
ISBN 0 946487 51 0 PBK £7.99

Luath Press Limited
committed to publishing well written books worth reading

LUATH PRESS takes its name from Robert Burns, whose little collie Luath (*Gael.*, swift or nimble) tripped up Jean Armour at a wedding and gave him the chance to speak to the woman who was to be his wife and the abiding love of his life. Burns called one of *The Twa Dogs* Luath after Cuchullin's hunting dog in *Ossian's Fingal*. Luath Press grew up in the heart of Burns country, and now resides a few steps up the road from Burns' first lodgings in Edinburgh's Royal Mile.

Luath offers you distinctive writing with a hint of unexpected pleasures.

Most UK bookshops either carry our books in stock or can order them for you. To order direct from us, please send a £sterling cheque, postal order, international money order or your credit card details (number, address of cardholder and expiry date) to us at the address below. Please add post and packing as follows: UK – £1.00 per delivery address; overseas surface mail – £2.50 per delivery address; overseas airmail – £3.50 for the first book to each delivery address, plus £1.00 for each additional book by airmail to the same address. If your order is a gift, we will happily enclose your card or message at no extra charge.

Luath Press Limited
543/2 Castlehill
The Royal Mile
Edinburgh EH1 2ND
Telephone: 0131 225 4326 (24 hours)
Fax: 0131 225 4324
email: gavin.macdougall@luath.co.uk
Website: www.luath.co.uk